THE RIGHT TO BE WRONG

THE RIGHT TO BE WRONG

*Ending the Culture War
over Religion in America*

Kevin Seamus Hasson

ENCOUNTER BOOKS
SAN FRANCISCO

First edition published in 2005 by Encounter Books, an activity of Encounter for Culture and Education, Inc., a nonprofit, tax exempt corporation.

Encounter Books website address: www.encounterbooks.com

Manufactured in the United States and printed on acid-free paper.

The paper used in this publication meets the minimum requirements of ANSI/NISO Z39.48-1992 (R 1997)(*Permanence of Paper*).

FIRST EDITION

Library of Congress Cataloging-in-Publication Data

Hasson, Kevin Seamus.
    The right to be wrong : religion and freedom in a pluralistic America / by Kevin Seamus Hasson.
       p. cm.
    ISBN 1-59403-083-9 (alk. paper)
1. Freedom of religion—United States. 2. Religious tolerance—United States. 3. United States—Religion.

BR516 .H33 2005
323.44'2'0973—dc22
2005019752

10 9 8 7 6 5 4 3 2 1

For Mary
(with a nod to G. C.)

Acknowledgments

Thanks to Heather Higgins for encouraging me to write this book. Thanks also to Craig Cardon for his invaluable help.

I owe several intellectual debts. While I have relied on many sources cited in the endnotes, I am especially in debt to Judge John Noonan for his scholarship in general and his work on Madison in particular. On the topic of Jefferson and slavery, I am indebted to Paul Finkelman. On Jefferson and religion, I owe at least a backhanded compliment to Isaac Kramnick and R. Laurence Moore, authors of *The Godless Constitution*, which gets many things wrong, but much about Jefferson right.

Both intellectually and practically, I am deeply indebted to Lori Halstead, from the Harvard Law School class of 2005, for her amazing combination of research and writing, not to mention her patience and good humor. I am similarly indebted to Austin Bramwell, from the Harvard Law School class of 2003, whose abilities are likewise prodigious. Thanks to Ben Dougherty, Notre Dame Law School class of 2007, for his invaluable assistance. Many thanks are also due to all my coworkers and friends at the Becket Fund, who contributed to this work in many ways through the years.

I am tremendously grateful to my wife, Mary, and my kids, who put up with me throughout this adventure. Thanks, lastly, to the fine folks at Starbucks #7526, where I wrote most of this.

Contents

Introduction ix

Part One: Learning the Hard Way

1
Of Pilgrims and Park Rangers
The extremists among us 1

2
Pluralism, Conscience and Community
Reflections on the Pilgrims' lack of progress 9

3
Religion in Public Culture
Reflections on Christmas in Plymouth Colony 21

4
What about Proselytizing?
Reflections on the Puritans' paranoia about dissent 29

5
Heavens No, We Won't Go
*Reflections on how the Quakers
invented conscientious objection* 45

6
Why Tolerance Is Intolerable
Reflections on the failure of the refuge colonies 57

Part Two: Groping for a Right

7
From Tolerance to Natural Rights
Reflections on the battle for disestablishment in Virginia 71

8
Inalienable Rights, Slightly Alienated
Reflections on Thomas Jefferson in public and in private 83

9
The Early First Amendment: A Disappointing Compromise
Reflections on Madison's greatest failure   95

10
In the States, the Aftermath of Compromise
*Reflections on legalized persecution
under the early First Amendment*   105

Part Three: Authentic Freedom

11
Where Does Religious Liberty Come From?
Reflections on who we are to deserve freedom   115

12
Personal, not Private
Reflections on why believers do it in public   125

13
The First Amendment at Midlife
*Reflections on the incorporation doctrine—and
how two wrongs make a right of uncertain scope*   131

14
The Right to Be Wrong
Ending the culture war   145

Notes   149

Index   171

Introduction

We've grown used to the trench warfare. Every December some group is suing to take both the Nativity scene and the menorah off the courthouse steps. Meanwhile another group is agitating to have one, but only one, of them put up. And it's not just holidays. It seems that no office of government, no matter how obscure, can conduct its affairs in peace without fear of a fight erupting between those who say that only their true religion belongs in public and those who say that no religions do. Most of us find ourselves caught in the middle, ducking for cover and wondering just who these people are and what could possibly make them tick.

Who are they? In this book we'll come to know them as the Pilgrims and the Park Rangers. Why "Pilgrims"? After the good but often obtuse people of Plymouth Colony. They thought only the truth was permissible in public and so they restricted other people's freedom. Why "Park Rangers"? After the well-intentioned but bumbling bureaucrats in a too-good-to-be-true story of New Agers, a public park, and a certain sacred parking barrier. For the Park Rangers, freedom requires driving away other people's truths, no matter how harmless. We will meet the Pilgrims and the Park Rangers and find out what makes them tick.

We'll find out also how to disarm them. Eleven years ago I founded the Becket Fund for Religious Liberty to help put a stop to the madness. The Becket Fund is a nonpartisan, interfaith, public-interest law firm that protects the free expression of all religious traditions, in America and around the world. To date we have successfully represented believers of nearly every tradition you can imagine: Jews, Christians, Muslims, Buddhists, Hindus, Sikhs, Native Americans and even Zoroastrians (you last knew them as the Magi). We are neither Pilgrims nor

Park Rangers. We defend all faiths but we are not relativists. On any given day, I think most of my clients are wrong. But I firmly believe that, in an important sense, they have the right to be wrong.

This book explains why. It is the fruit of my eleven years of contending with both Pilgrims and Park Rangers in courts domestic and international, and debating them in venues stretching from Harvard Law School to the Vatican, from the *Today* show to Al-Jazeera.

The book touches on both law and history but it's neither a legal treatise nor a historical tome. It is about religious liberty but it is not a religious book. In fact, it can't be. A religious argument for religious liberty in America would convince, at most, those Americans who believed in that religion. It would likely be counterproductive with some others. Instead, this is a book of stories—some funny, some ironic, some tragic—featuring characters ranging from the heroic to the hapless to the homicidal. A few of the stories are well known; most are not. They are arranged more or less chronologically. They skewer any number of sacred cows. Reflecting on them exposes the Pilgrims and the Park Rangers for the extremists they are and points the way to ending their trench warfare. It lets us see that freedom for all of us is based on the truth about each of us.

Part One

Learning the Hard Way

ONE

Of Pilgrims and Park Rangers

The extremists among us

It is perhaps America's most enduring myth: The Pilgrims came here looking for religious freedom, found it, and we all lived happily ever after.

They weren't. They didn't. We haven't.

As we'll see, the Pilgrims actually came here looking mostly for real estate. They were a quirky, if courageous little band of religious separatists. And like religious separatists before them and since—from the authors of the Dead Sea Scrolls to the monks of the Egyptian desert to the Amish of today—they wanted nothing so much as to be left alone to live in their own world according to their own vision of the truth. They came to America not because it offered freedom for all but simply because it offered a refuge for them.

The problem was, other people kept showing up. Even aboard the *Mayflower* there were the "strangers," whom the Pilgrims' English investors had insisted accompany them. Then, after they'd established Plymouth Colony, more ships brought more strangers. As we'll also see, the Pilgrims did not respond well to this unplanned pluralism. In fact, they attempted to outlaw it. They set up tax-supported churches and banned competing religious services or cultural displays. They kept dissidents from proselytizing. They had religious tests for public office. And they refused to exempt conscientious objectors, like Quakers, from obeying their laws.

We haven't lived happily ever after, either. We have, of course, come a long way since the Pilgrims first measured out their stingy

1

servings of tolerance. Nevertheless, the fundamental problem that the Pilgrims and the strangers faced when confronted with each other is still with us: How do you reconcile claims of absolute truth with human freedom in a pluralistic society?

In fact, that problem is not only still with us, it is growing ever more serious as our society grows ever more pluralistic— and as the extremists on both sides grow ever more polarized. It has reached the point where we aptly call the whole imbroglio one of the culture wars.

How to resolve it? We must begin by understanding it. So let's meet the combatants.

In this corner, wearing the funny hats...the Pilgrims

On the one hand there are still many Pilgrims among us, people who want to use the state to coerce the religious consciences of those with whom they disagree. For these latter-day Pilgrims the relationship of truth and freedom seems every bit as straightforward as it did to their namesakes in Plymouth Colony: The truth is, well, true. So how, they demand to know, can they *not* seek to establish it legally? If they don't, won't they be conceding that they harbor some doubts after all? And even if they did succeed in legally establishing the true religion, would that be such a bad thing? Wouldn't they really just be doing a favor to the not-yet-enlightened by hastening the day when their eyes are opened?

Most Americans instinctively recoil from such logic. We know it can't be right. We may or may not know how to parse the philosophical mistake involved, but we're sure there must be one in there somewhere. We know that religious truth cannot be embraced authentically unless it is embraced freely. To American ears, the idea that truth is somehow opposed to freedom rings false. Pilgrims are obviously extremists.

And in this corner, wearing the hapless expressions... the Park Rangers

But Pilgrims aren't the only extremists. On the other hand there are the Park Rangers, who insist—even after the tragedies of the last century—that only a society that owns no truth at all can be safe for freedom. For them, the price of freedom for everyone is that no one can be allowed to publicly claim that anything transcendent is absolutely true. Why call them "Park Rangers"? In honor of a particularly memorable example of their zeal. Perry Mason might have called it "The Case of the Sacred Parking Barrier."

It all began in the Japanese Tea Garden of San Francisco's Golden Gate Park in 1989. The tea garden had long been a particularly well-groomed part of the park, a haven from the stresses of urban life. That year, however, there was a problem. A crane operator had abandoned a traffic or parking barrier at the back of the tea garden. It was a small, bullet-shaped lump of granite that clashed with the ordered nature of the place, an irritant that park-goers periodically tried to have removed. Bureaucrats being what they are, however, the stray parking barrier remained.

It remained, that is, until 1993, when the bureaucrats learned of a New Age group's interest in it. The New Agers, it seemed, had recognized something significant about the shape of the parking barrier: It resembled a Shiva Lingam, a manifestation of the Hindu god Shiva. What was more, they had come upon it unexpectedly and in a wooded setting, just the way you're supposed to discover a Shiva Lingam. The little band of believers had rejoiced and begun to worship. In fact, they now came regularly to pray and make offerings of incense and flowers to the stone bullet. All of which greatly alarmed the very same authorities (with a little poetic license, the "Park Rangers") who had resolutely neglected to remove the traffic barrier as an eyesore. The bureaucrats roused themselves and announced that it was their duty to prevent worship on (not to mention of) public property; the parking barrier had to go.

Whereupon, the New Agers promptly got a lawyer and sued for an order blocking removal of the little granite lump. The case settled two months later, in January 1994. Rather than spend time and money in court, the authorities agreed to give the spare barrier to its devotees, who agreed to pray to it in private, someplace else.

Now, as lawsuits go this was hardly a legal landmark. After

all, the parking barrier really was public property and the authorities always were free to do with it as they pleased. As an account of religion in public life, however, the case is something of a parable. If ever there was a religion that was not threatening, either politically or culturally, this had to be it. Nobody could ever have mistaken parking-barrier worship for an officially established religion, even in San Francisco. No one could really have wondered whether it would be politically correct to be seen leaving flowers in front of the thing. Nobody could honestly worry that tax money might be spent on incense for it. In short, this particular piece of religious expression did not remotely threaten to coerce anyone to do anything. What's more, the tea garden was a public park. If people could come to admire the shrubbery, why couldn't they come to worship the parking barriers?

Because, said the authorities, parking-barrier worship was religion and religion didn't belong on public property. Religion belonged in private. It was just that simple.

There are many Park Rangers among us, from zoning commissioners to school administrators to...actual park rangers. And they all seem to think it's just that simple. They come out in force at the holidays. Controversies over Christmas Nativity scenes and Hanukkah menorahs have, of course, become a yearly ritual. But the battle lines have moved far beyond them. There are now annual debates over a variety of cultural offerings. Some Park Rangers, stung by criticism that the Easter Bunny isn't already a secular enough symbol, have made over the little creature as best they can. For example, the public school system in Lansing, Michigan, now offers, in lieu of Easter, a "Breakfast with the Special Bunny." And, until nearly everyone laughed at it, the public library in Arlington, Virginia, had replaced its annual Easter Egg Hunt with a "Spring Egg Roll." Other places have banned in-school celebrations of Halloween, on one of two conflicting theories: either because it's an inappropriately Catholic celebration of All Hallows' Eve, or else because it's an inappropriately pagan celebration of something else. At least one school system has banned Valentine's Day because it's named after Saint Valentine. The kids can still send each other notes, though they can't call them valentines. They have to call them "special person cards."

What drives these people? Some are devout deconstructionists. That is, they are convinced that there really is no such thing as objective truth at all. Most Park Rangers, though, are not. Most, ever so privately, believe in something or other. But they're Park Rangers still. Why? Because they think that freedom is incompatible with public claims of any religious truth—even their own. All religion, they insist, must be purely private. And just why is that? It's largely because they're afraid of the Pilgrims.

To hear the Park Rangers tell it, the West is free because Westerners are mostly easygoing folk, untainted by fanatical devotion to absolute truths. Columnist Andrew Sullivan memorably made this case in his fierce post-9/11 *New York Times Magazine* cover article, "This Is a Religious War." Sullivan framed the war against al-Qaeda and other anti-American terrorist groups as a conflict between two kinds of religion: It is "a war of fundamentalism against faiths of all kinds that are at peace with freedom and modernity." He charged that belief in absolute truth, which he seemed to equate with "fundamentalism," inevitably produces coercion. "If you believe that there is an eternal afterlife and that endless indescribable torture awaits those who disobey God's law, then it requires no huge stretch of imagination to make sure that you not only conform to each diktat but that you also encourage and, if necessary, coerce others to do the same.... In a world of absolute truth, in matters graver than life and death, there is no room for dissent and no room for theological doubt." In other words, only uncertainty can save us from the killing fields. The only good religion is a relativist one.

What to do, then, with all those recalcitrant religions that insist they really do possess the truth? The Park Rangers' answer is simple: Push them out of public life and keep them as culturally marginal as possible. Replace all that messy competition with a wrinkle-free, synthetic, one-size-fits-all culture.

As we'll see, that's literally inhuman.

It's also self-defeating. It doesn't resolve the culture war; it enflames it. It alarms the Pilgrims every bit as much as their sermons frighten the Park Rangers. So both sides take to their direct-mail houses to quote each other and amass bigger war chests by sowing further anxiety. Each ends up being the other's best fundraiser and worst bogeyman.

(The Park Rangers' position is counterproductive in a subtler way as well. Barring public truth claims about who God is often morphs into barring public truth claims about who we are. Yet truth claims about ourselves are what human rights are based on. Barring such truth claims in the name of freedom is like sawing off the limb you're sitting on.)

In short, the Park Rangers' solution to pluralism is as defective as the Pilgrims' is. In their drive to prevent theocracy, the Park Rangers end up promoting a society that is insufficiently human—and is at least as divided as the one they're trying to forestall.

This Way Out

It sometimes seems we are condemned to an endless tug-of-war between Pilgrims and Park Rangers and we dare not let either side win. If the Pilgrims prevail, both freedom of conscience and civil society diminish. We will have once again the gray hypocrisy of government-imposed orthodoxy. If the Park Rangers win, we risk having only the sort of temporary, politically based religious liberty that has proven so inadequate throughout much of the world. And we will certainly have a vapid public culture. We will be nervous for our rights in the midst of one vast, unending Breakfast with the Special Bunny.

Either way, religious freedom suffers. But it, and we, suffer from the ongoing struggle as well. Must this be? Not if we can rise above the impasse. To do this, we must be able to guarantee a robust religious freedom for all—and not just for some—and base it on something that's undeniable to both Pilgrims and Park Rangers. That is, we must ground religious freedom for all in something more universally convincing than the parochial truth claims of the Pilgrims, but do it without contradicting those truth claims. We must guarantee the Park Rangers (and everyone else) their freedom of conscience, grounding it in something far firmer than just their own anxieties, while not unduly aggravating those anxieties. That is our challenge and also the subject of this book.

We'll approach it by considering a series of stories. In the rest of Part One, we'll highlight the big questions of religious liberty by telling the stories of the early colonists' blunders—some earnest, some hapless, some funny, and some tragic. They shed light on the origins of pluralism and the tension between conscience and community, on the question of religious expression in public culture, on the perennial controversy over proselytism, and on the issue of conscientious objection to law. We'll end Part One with stories of the best idea that the colonies came up with to deal with those questions—and how it wasn't then, and isn't now, good enough. That is, we'll see why tolerance, as nice as it sounds, has always been an inadequate basis for religious liberty.

In Part Two, we'll tell the story of how an inkling grew into an idea and then lost its way. The story begins with the adventures, and misadventures, of James Madison and Thomas Jefferson as they started to argue for a religious freedom based on human nature. The story continues with tales of the compromises that crept in as religious liberty was then codified in the United States Constitution. It ends with the religious riots and legalized persecutions that followed.

In Part Three, we'll return to first principles and propose an updated model of religious liberty that both remains faithful to its origins and transcends the extremists' running feud. It points the way to a pluralism both honest and untidy, but firmly grounded. And we'll tell some good stories there, too.

Throughout, we'll maintain a running critique of the Pilgrims and the Park Rangers among us. (We just have to refute them; we don't have to make them comfortable.)

We'll start with the story of the arguments aboard the *Mayflower,* for the light it sheds on where pluralism comes from. So the saga really does begin with the Pilgrims after all. But it begins with the real Pilgrims, not the mythical ones.

TWO

Pluralism, Conscience and Community

Reflections on the Pilgrims' lack of progress

The saints and the strangers were arguing. The "saints" (what the Pilgrims called themselves) were insisting that the "strangers" (what they called the non-Pilgrims aboard the *Mayflower*) yield to their vision of how life should be when they reached America. The strangers were having none of it.

It was an omen, of sorts.

Religious pluralism has been a fact of life in America ever since. America is now home to a broad assortment of people who believe a wide variety of things to be true. We all, naturally, want to embrace our beliefs openly and in community with our fellow believers. At the same time, however, we all have to live with each other. That is, we have to live with people who want to embrace different, competing beliefs just as openly and in community with *their* fellow believers. But how can our competing communities be in community with each other in society at large? How can you live with people who are dead certain that you're wrong about matters of eternal significance—especially when you're just as certain that you're not wrong at all, but they are?

We can learn how *not* to do it—and *why* not—from the original Pilgrims' most basic mistake. That means, of course, that their halos will require some adjusting.

Who Are These Guys?

The self-described Pilgrims who founded Plymouth Colony in

1620 Massachusetts, and who are the heroes of many a Thanks-giving Day pageant, were a small splinter group of separatist Puritans who had broken with the Church of England some fourteen years earlier. Puritans in general were English Protes-tants who thought the Reformation there hadn't gone far enough. They wanted to purify the Anglican church of what they saw as its Catholic trappings and its moral and spiritual decay. Most Puritans thought of themselves simply as dissenting Anglicans. Separatists, on the other hand, were a minority of hardliners who believed the Church of England to be so abom-inably corrupt that they had no choice but to abandon it lest they be defiled, too. Because breaking with the established church was against the law, a number of the separatists decided to flee.

Their first choice of refuge was not America. Rather, they fled to Holland, where they found all the tolerance they wanted—and then some. Ten years later, when a young William Bradford helped lead a tiny band of them to America, they were no longer fleeing persecution, but permissiveness. Not only were they being tolerated, they were being assimilated. Their children were making friends with the locals, whose mores were not up to Pilgrim standards. In the words of Bradford, "many of their children, by...a great licentiousness of youth in that country, and the manifold temptations of the place, were drawn away by evil examples...." The most radical of the Pilgrims decided they must, once again, pull up stakes and leave.

Their second choice of refuge was not America, either. The Jamestown Settlement in Virginia was officially Anglican, and so out of the question (the law there even required attendance at daily prayer services). Instead, they seriously considered Guyana. They decided against that, finally, because of concerns about the climate and worries about a future Spanish conquest. Reconsidering America, they wondered whether they could count on toleration of their separatist faith if they established a new English colony distinct from Jamestown. The king refused any formal toleration but signaled that he would nevertheless look the other way.

And so it happened that in 1620 a minority of the Holland

community—a splinter group of a splinter group—decided to make for America aboard the *Mayflower.* Most members of the church remained behind, with only 35 Pilgrims deciding to leave. They were joined by some 40 of their fellow separatists from England and about 25 others who were not separatists at all, but workers foisted upon the group by its financial backers in London. The result was a sometimes-prickly voyage aboard the *Mayflower* as the two factions (which the Pilgrims undiplomatically dubbed "saints" and "strangers") squabbled.

Getting Along (Sort of)

Pluralism had broken out and no one knew quite what to do about it. Imagine the Pilgrims' frustration. They had fled England for Holland, and then Holland for the wilderness, just to get away from impurity—and impurity had tagged along. Now what were they going to do? Imagine, too, the strangers' discomfort. They were ordinary people who had left their country, not for deep spiritual reasons, but simply because this was the best job they could find. And here they were, stuck with a bunch of holier-than-thou zealots who promised to be no fun at all. How could they possibly all live together?

There, in miniature, is the question we still face: How to live together despite the most profound differences over what life means in the first place? The Pilgrims would offer a singularly unimaginative answer. But not before the question grew more acute.

When the *Mayflower* finally spotted land, saints and strangers alike found themselves seriously off course and over two hundred miles from their land grant. This presented several problems, not the least of which was who, if anyone, had the legal authority to be in charge. The outnumbered strangers, to their evident relief, at first said nobody did. But anarchy in the wilderness was no answer. Like it or not, they were all in this together. They would have to reach some sort of accommodation.

That was the Mayflower Compact, a sort of proto-constitution for the fledgling colony. The compact gave the colonists a great opportunity to experiment with self-government. And the Pilgrims took some advantage of it, creating significantly new political structures. But not having sought religious freedom, they would not have religious freedom thrust upon them. They had no intention of imitating the broad tolerance they had received in Holland. Nor did they wish to extend to anyone else even the same informal tolerance they presently enjoyed from the Crown. No, there were more saints than strangers and that would be that. They used their political power to establish tax-supported churches, ban competing ones, and require church membership as a condition for holding public office.

(Many point out that the ideas of self-government and freedom of religion are connected, that the Mayflower Compact ended up making "enduring contributions to the heritage of religious liberty." No doubt. But if the Pilgrims had known that was what they were doing, they would have solemnly repented.)

The compact didn't resolve the question of pluralism; it just reformulated it. As soon as the struggling little colony got up and going, with the Pilgrims firmly in charge, the question returned again and again: How much dissent would the Pilgrims tolerate?

The consistent answer was, not much.

Never Had a Prayer

In 1624, for example, Plymouth banished John Lyford, an Anglican minister sent over by the colony's financial backers in England. What had he done? Among other things, he and his friends, "without ever speaking one word either to the Governor, Church, or Elder, withdrew themselves and set up a public meeting apart on the Lord's Day."

Now, wanting to publicly embrace the truth as one knows it is natural enough. That's why the Pilgrims themselves didn't just believe privately at home. We don't believe in private because we don't live in private. We humans are social creatures. If something is important to us we naturally want to celebrate it, or mourn it, together with others. We don't smuggle babies home from the hospital; we have showers and brises and baptisms. We don't come of age in secret; we have bar mitzvahs and bat mitzvahs, confirmations and coming-out parties. We don't marry in secret, but spend months (and fortunes) planning weddings. And we don't furtively bury our dead; we conduct funerals where we can weep together. We don't live alone; we live together.

Faith is very much like that. The great stories of generations of persecuted peoples keeping their traditions alive in secret are heroic precisely because that effort requires something humanly extraordinary. The normal thing to do is to join with others and embrace our beliefs openly and in community.

For Governor Bradford, however, permitting a rival, Anglican community in Plymouth making rival truth claims was simply unimaginable. Like the legally established Anglicans from whom they had originally fled, the legally established Pilgrims would brook no separatism.

The utter shamelessness with which Bradford reports banishing an Anglican who wished to separate from the separatists—that is, who wanted to do in Plymouth precisely what the Pilgrims themselves had done in England—is instructive. This is not just obtuseness or garden-variety ingratitude. It's a very conscious double standard between the Pilgrims' true religion and everybody else's false ones. The truth was entitled to freedom, whether in England or Holland, Guyana or Plymouth. The same could not be said, however, for false religions, which were to be legally suppressed wherever possible. Accordingly, it would be a good thing for the misguided Anglicans to tolerate the truthful Pilgrims. But it would be a bad thing for the Pilgrims, once in power, to tolerate them.

In 1658, when the colony revamped its legal code, the preamble codified that notion. It stressed that civil authorities, who received their power from God, must use it for "the upholding of his worship and services and against the contrary."

What about conscience? After all they'd been through, wouldn't separatists, of all people, defer to someone's conscience? Well, "due respect" was to be given to those "differing and dissenting in some smaller matters" (that is, to those with consciences close enough for government work). But anyone professing a belief that "tends to...the overthrow of the churches of God or of his worship" had to be dealt with. Dissenters' consciences, in other words, would be tolerated only insofar as they required something trivial. If they ever organized communities that competed with the legally established religion, the government would have to quash them.

The Pilgrims' response to the question of pluralism was thus vintage seventeenth century. How do you live together with religious dissenters? You live together with religious dissenters by repressing them. The truth requires you to restrict their freedom, conscience or no conscience.

That was a fundamental misunderstanding of conscience—and it led to a fundamental misunderstanding of pluralism. It is a misunderstanding that plagues us still.

It's Only Human

Conscience is the interior, quintessentially human voice that speaks to us of goodness and duty, the voice we must obey if we are to keep our integrity. It counsels doing good and avoiding evil, and serves as a referee to rule on which is which. What is more, conscience requires action, not just conviction. It demands that we live according to the truth as we know it.

Conscience, of course, is neither omniscient nor infallible. It needs an education, though even with one it still makes mistakes. But, as fallible and ignorant as conscience may sometimes be, it's in charge and it knows it. It takes the truth, as we understand it, and applies it to real-life problems to judge what's good. To refuse to follow its judgment (even if it later turns out to have been mistaken) is to consciously reject what we believe to be true and turn our backs on what we believe to be good.

Now, if the world were perfect, everyone would agree on what the truth is and all our consciences would be pulling in the same direction. In the flawed and imperfect world that really exists, however, this is not the case. Even the brightest minds, the biggest hearts and the best-educated, most tuned-in consciences can and do differ. Yet they all must be obeyed. The odds of unanimity on life's important questions—including religious observance—are thus very long.

Which brings us to pluralism. Pluralism results more or less inevitably from these three facts about conscience: It's not infallible but it is in charge—and it demands action, not just belief. An interior voice that is often right, sometimes wrong, but always authoritative will predictably lead different people to embrace the different religious convictions they believe to be true, and to live accordingly.

Religious diversity is thus a fact of life. It is neither good nor bad in itself. It can't be outlawed and needn't be glorified. It simply is. The question isn't how to maximize diversity, nor how to minimize it. The question is how to live authentically in the midst of it, while allowing others to do the same. That is, how to seek, express and embrace authentically what we are convinced is the true and the good, while allowing others to seek, express and embrace authentically what we are convinced is the mistaken and inadequate.

Pluralism without Relativism

A large part of the answer, which the good people of Plymouth missed, is respect for conscience. We can, and should, respect others' duty to follow their consciences even as we insist that they're mistaken. Why? Because others have the same duty to follow their presumably mistaken consciences as we do to follow our presumably correct ones.

Wouldn't that make us all relativists? No. Respect for conscience makes sense of clashing truth claims without denying them or relativizing them. It's not that there is no truth, as the deconstructionists would have it, or that everything is somehow true for somebody, as the greeting-card writers would. It's that people make mistakes about what the truth is, yet still have to obey their consciences nonetheless. So we can respect their duty to follow their consciences and embrace a particular faith— and at the very same time be utterly convinced that the faith they're embracing is absolute drivel.

Put differently, respecting people's duty to follow their consciences doesn't necessarily imply that we think their beliefs might actually be true. Recall the "Case of the Sacred Parking

Barrier" from the first chapter. Hardly anyone thinks it's even remotely possible that the parking barrier might really be God. There is no sense pretending otherwise. But bemusedly respecting the worshippers' duty to obey their highly unusual consciences is a different matter. Integrity is always honorable, even in an eccentric.

Yet doesn't this prove too much? What do we do with the truly bad conscience, the sort that's bent on doing harm, and how do we know where to draw the line? It's been said that foolproof plans don't take into account the ingenuity of fools. Something similar could be said of religious liberty. Let's face it: some people plot destruction in the name of religion. They may be sincerely following their very warped consciences, but they are very real dangers to society nonetheless. What do we do with those whose consciences can't be accommodated?

We stop them, of course. We deter them where possible and prosecute them where necessary. Religious liberty is not absolute. That's the easy part of the question.

The crucial, and hard, part of the question is at what point do we draw the line? How do we know when we can't accommodate? The point is not (as some Park Rangers would have us believe) the moment when people begin to disagree. Nor is it the point where we see expressions of religions we believe to be false in the public square. Nor is it even the point at which we must tolerate some inconvenience for the sake of someone else's conscience—being stuck behind an Amish buggy on the highway, for example. Those are examples of normal pluralism, not unhealthy coercion. As we'll discuss later in more detail, the point where the government should step in is the point where the government *must* step in to protect its citizens, the point where an allegedly religious practice begins to disrupt public health, safety and morals. Government should intervene when (and only when) it's necessary to protect the public from a here-and-now menace, rather than from the spiritual effects of heresy.

Some Still Don't Have a Prayer

Respect for conscience, and for the pluralism that results from

it, at its most basic, requires allowing those with whom we disagree to form their communities, to gather and worship
together. This is so even if, as was the case with John Lyford's
followers in Plymouth, those communities dissent from the
tenets of the community as a whole.

Now, this may seem an obvious point, and Plymouth's banishing of Lyford for holding dissident worship services an
equally obvious failing. But these points are not obvious at all to
either the Pilgrims or the Park Rangers among us. Both still
want to use the government to restrict public worship that they
find distasteful.

Perhaps the best, and highest-profile, example is Hialeah,
Florida. In 1987, officials there opposed the practice of Santeria,
a primitive Cuban folk religion, in their city. Responding to
pressure from more mainstream religions, they outlawed Santeria rituals by prohibiting the "sacrifice" of animals within city
limits. The Supreme Court struck down the ban, observing that
you could legally kill animals in any number of ways in
Hialeah—you could hunt them, fish them, trap them and, if
they were lobsters, boil them alive; the only thing you couldn't
do was "sacrifice" them, that is, kill them for a religious reason.
And that, the Court noted, was obviously an effort to prevent
the practice of a disfavored faith.

Lower-level Pilgrims attempt to enforce the truth as well.
The Cobb County Jail in Georgia is a good example. In 1998,
authorities there wouldn't let Catholic priests minister to prisoners. After the threat of a Becket Fund lawsuit, they
relented—but then forbade any Catholic baptisms. Following a
renewed threat, they finally gave in. It seemed one of the jailers
believed that Catholics weren't real Christians and was using his
position to protect the prisoners from heresy.

Public worship isn't threatened just by Pilgrims, though.
Equally misguided, but perhaps less clumsy, are the efforts
of many Park Rangers to protect the public from religious services generally. Westchester County, New York, tried in 2002 to
forbid eleven Buddhists from meditating together in a private
home because, authorities said, it lacked special zoning. Turns
out that religion in a residential neighborhood is unsettling.

(Among other things, the bureaucrats said they were concerned that the silent meditation could produce too much noise. Some legal briefs just write themselves.) That same year, the city of Cypress, California, attempted to condemn eighteen acres that an evangelical church had purchased to build its sanctuary. The government wanted the land to go to Costco instead. Seems that religion in too prominent a place isn't acceptable, either. (The Becket Fund persuaded a federal court to enjoin the attempted land grab.) And zoning officials in Grand Haven, Michigan, refused to let a storefront church rent a storefront. Religion in a commercial district? Bad for business. (They settled a Becket Fund lawsuit with a consent decree.)

These are not isolated examples. As of this writing, the Becket Fund has over a dozen similar cases pending around the country, on behalf of a wide variety of faiths.

Déjà Vu

Plymouth's most basic mistake was that it gave "due respect" only to consciences "differing and dissenting in some smaller matters" from the prevailing line. Consequently it failed to respect the pluralism that results from dissenting consciences. Pilgrims and Park Rangers alike make the same mistake. When Pilgrims get their way, only some religions can worship publicly. The rest literally don't have a prayer, or at least not a public one. When Park Rangers are running the show, on the other hand, all houses of worship are equally unwelcome—uptown, downtown or in the suburbs. Both sides misunderstand pluralism because neither has respect for conscience.

But…"respect for conscience"? That's it? You expect us to call off the culture war just because somebody tells us to "respect" each other? What can that possibly mean—where does it begin and end? Don't all these confused and wrong-headed people I'm supposed to respect have to respect me, too? And what about the law—do they get to disregard it in favor of their precious consciences? Always, sometimes, never? And how in the world can we possibly know? Important questions that we'll consider through the lens of the stories that follow.

The next story reveals another mistake that endures to the present. This story, though, verges on the slapstick. What might Dr. Seuss, Charles Dickens and William Bradford's *Journal* all have in common?

THREE

Religion in Public Culture

Reflections on Christmas in Plymouth Colony

They didn't say "humbug." But then they weren't really scrooges. The Pilgrims banned Christmas not to keep people from having fun. (Really.) They banned it because they didn't believe in Christmas themselves and they couldn't stand to have a holiday they disagreed with being celebrated in public.

Why should they? After all, it was their culture; and they had the legal authority to ban holidays if they wanted to. Why should they let dissidents do something as culturally potent as celebrating Christmas?

Almost four hundred years later, that's still a question in the minds of some Pilgrims and Park Rangers. In fact, it's an even bigger question now that a broader assortment of religions want to celebrate a wider variety of beliefs. "Sure," the extremists say, "out of respect for conscience, we may have to let them all gather in their communities and worship. But what about things that aren't limited to life *inside* their communities? What about things like holiday celebrations and displays, and religious music and art—things that extend *out* of their religious communities into the culture at large? Do we have to put up with them, too?"

The story of Christmas in Plymouth lets us reflect on just that question.

Plymouth as Whoville

In Plymouth, culture was served up in one simple, strong flavor:

21

Pilgrim. Their holidays were no exception. They were minimalist affairs, limited to what the Pilgrims thought could be adapted from ancient Israel. They rigorously observed Sunday, which they referred to as the Sabbath. They declared ad hoc days of humiliation and fasting on the one hand, and days of thanksgiving on the other, and they held a harvest celebration— all in imitation of the Israelites. These were their holidays and these were *all* their holidays. Just because there may have been room to spare in their culture didn't mean just anybody could fill it.

The difference between October and December 1621 is a telling illustration. In October the Pilgrims held what has come to be mythologized as the First Thanksgiving. It seems to have been a combination of their harvest festival and one of their occasionally proclaimed days of thanks. In any event, it was particularly boisterous by Pilgrim standards. It lasted several days and featured marksmanship contests and "other recreations," in addition to food (thereby setting the precedent for both turkey and football). In short, it was as communal and festive as Pilgrims could ever be.

Two months later, however, on "the day called Christmas Day, the Governor called them out to work," Bradford wrote in his *Journal*. That was normal. For Pilgrims, December 25 was a day just like any other. Christmas, they thought, was a "papist" innovation. Unlike their feast days, you couldn't find it in the Bible, so they wouldn't celebrate it. The previous year, they had spent their first Christmas in Plymouth splitting lumber.

But this time not everyone agreed. Some newly arrived colonists objected that "it went against their consciences to work" on Christmas. So Governor Bradford grudgingly excused them "till they were better informed" and led the wiser, more veteran colonists away to work.

Returning at noon, however, he was horrified to discover the newcomers "in the street at play, openly" engaged in various sports. That is, the newcomers were doing exactly what the Pilgrims had done two months earlier. But this was different. This wasn't a Pilgrim-proclaimed holiday; this was that papist invention, Christ's Mass. The governor knew what he had to do. He confiscated their sports equipment, telling them that if they insisted on celebrating Christmas as a "matter of devotion" they could do so privately in their houses, "but there should be no gaming or reveling in the streets." And so began, and quickly ended, the opening battle in the culture war over public celebrations of Christmas in America.

It was no isolated tantrum. A generation later, the colony formally outlawed Christmas for twenty-two years. (The English Puritans, when they seized power there under Cromwell, did the same and Christmas in England went underground. One result was the carol "The Twelve Days of Christmas," which sang in code—partridges in pear trees and so forth—of the twelve outlawed church feast days between Christmas and Epiphany.)

There is no record of what the Christmas revelers in Plymouth did after they lost their sports gear. We don't know whether they composed their own cryptic songs, if they met secretly to drink furtive Christmas toasts, or if they did something else to vindicate their consciences. But even as it is, the episode is instructive.

Note again the Pilgrims' double standard. Only two months before they suppressed the Christmas revelers, the Pilgrims had held their own gaming and reveling for an official harvest celebration. They knew after all that it's only natural for people to want to celebrate special times together. A holiday spent in enforced privacy is no holiday at all. Who ever heard of reveling alone?

It's likewise only natural for people celebrating something to want to express themselves to the world at large about it. That's what fireworks are all about. And parades, and decorations, and costumes. Why did the newcomers have to revel in the streets? Because they were happy it was Christmas and they wanted everyone to know it. Reveling is and always has been a public activity. (Which is why "reveling in the streets" is a catchphrase and "reveling in the basement" isn't.)

But what was good for the true culture of the Pilgrims was different from what was good for the erroneous culture of

Christmas. It was good for the Pilgrims to celebrate the truth in public. But it was also good for the Pilgrims not to be offended by different and confusingly winsome cultural displays. So it was good for Christmas to be suppressed.

Note, more fundamentally, the way Bradford reacted to the revelers' appeal to conscience. Initially when they had said that it violated their consciences to work, they were excused, albeit reluctantly. But that was when Bradford assumed that their consciences required them to do only what a misinformed Pilgrim might do on Christmas—pray privately. When it turned out that what their consciences had in mind was celebrating publicly, all bets were off. Once again, for William Bradford and his Pilgrims, dissenting consciences were tolerable in private but not in public. You could be privately happy it was Christmas; you just couldn't celebrate it publicly.

Bradford once again missed the point about conscience. Conscience tells us we must embrace what we believe to be true. But it tells us to embrace it as human beings embrace things, not as a computer might. That is, we must embrace the truth as we know it, not just intellectually, but with our personalities.

Now there are truths and there are truths. Some don't exactly lend themselves to exuberance. Nobody but a postdoc, for example, would toast the Pythagorean Theorem. But when embracing a truth includes celebrating it, that means "reveling in the streets," not just dryly noting its existence. For Plymouth's Christmas revelers, the truth was that at a moment in time, in Jesus of Nazareth, God had become man. The day they annually commemorated that moment had come. So of course "it went against their consciences to work" on Christmas. It wasn't time for work; it was time to celebrate. Their consciences insisted that they observe Christmas; their social natures insisted on how—by reveling in the streets.

The 400 Years War

Even after nearly four hundred years, we're still fighting the holiday wars—and still missing the same point Bradford did about conscience. We're still debating whether to allow religious holidays into public culture. Only now the holidays in question are even more diverse than Christmas seemed in Plymouth. Now they're from entirely distinct religions. And they each want what Plymouth's Christmas revelers wanted—to share their joy in public.

Pilgrims and Park Rangers alike find that prospect worrisome. A variety of religious celebrations seems to both extremes to be just too volatile a mix to be released into the culture.

Pilgrims fear that people will be seduced by a rival worldview, and so are every bit as insistent about censoring cultural celebrations as their Plymouth namesakes were. The government, they think, should recognize only their true holidays and be banned from recognizing other, false ones. The argument is often dressed up as a constitutional one—"the First Amendment permits my display in City Hall but unfortunately forbids yours." That pitch has been tried in every possible permutation: Nativity-scenes-but-not-menorahs, menorahs-but-not-Nativity-scenes, even the-solstice-but-neither-menorahs-nor-Nativity-scenes. (No, not California; New Jersey, 1997.) In all cases, the conclusion is vintage Pilgrim: The truth is allowed in official, public culture, while other, deviant holidays must be celebrated only in private.

It is the Park Rangers, though, who are the most relentless censors of public holidays on the contemporary scene. Where Pilgrims are truth-at-all-costs zealots of one persuasion or another, Park Rangers are equal-opportunity oppressors who seek, in the name of freedom, to exclude all religious elements of culture, whatever the underlying faith might be. They want the culture homogenized and bland. (If there had been Park Rangers in Plymouth, their solution to Christmas would have been to ban Thanksgiving, too.)

Some Park Rangers go right for the jugular. They seek simply to outlaw government recognition of religious holidays in the first place. Acting on such a complaint in *Metzl v. Leininger*, the U.S. Court of Appeals for the Seventh Circuit struck down Good Friday as an official holiday in Illinois. The judges said that closing the government on Good Friday was an improper endorsement of religion. (A different panel of judges from the same court later upheld Indiana's Good Friday holiday because, they said, it was different. Indiana wasn't trying to be religious at all; it just wanted a long weekend off during the spring and this was as good as any. They didn't quote, though they might have, the army press officer who said it was "necessary to destroy the village in order to save it.") As of this writing, there have been at least a dozen lawsuits around the country challenging various holidays—Yom Kippur (*ACLU v. Sycamore Community School District*), Christmas (*Ganulin v. United States*), Easter (*Bonham v. District of Columbia Library Admin.*), Good Friday (*Brindenbaugh v. O'Bannon; Granzier v. Middleton*), and more.

And every December some Park Ranger somewhere will be suing to try to force the Nativity scene and the menorah off the courthouse steps (and the Becket Fund will be defending both).

The Park Rangers' preferred strategy, though, is proactive: It is to invent new, inherently meaningless holidays to replace the old, religiously based ones. You can always tell when Park Rangers are in charge. In December the place will be celebrating only "the winter holidays" or, in Pittsburgh until recently, "Sparkle Season." Hanukkah and Christmas will be purely private affairs. (One panicky Ohio bureaucrat in 2003 even said with a straight face that the tree they'd decorated that December was really for Pearl Harbor Day.)

Similar things happen from a kids'-eye view in public schools. As we saw in Chapter One, Halloween becomes the "Fall Festival," Saint Valentine's Day morphs into "Special Person Day," and Easter mutates into "Special Bunny Day."

Still Missing the Point

These efforts are every bit as small-minded as the original Pilgrims' efforts were. It is, first of all, naïve to imagine that bureaucrats can simply invent new traditions that will be as aesthetically satisfying as those built up over centuries. Sparkle Seasons will always taste half-baked.

Second, and more fundamentally, the Park Rangers misunderstand holidays' role in culture. Holiday celebrations are not just days off; they are community celebrations of something we value, whether it's ethnicity (Saint Patrick's Day), heroism (Veterans' Day), religion (Hanukkah, Christmas, etc.), or just the passage of time (New Year's). And no one values "sparkling" for its own sake. In our holidays we tell the world something of who we are.

The same is true of our arts. Architecture, when it's good, expresses to the outside world what it mirrors to the people inside the building: their community, what they have in common that leads them to gather there in the first place. Our music does, too. From the national anthem to school fight songs to Broadway to pop, it embodies something of our common identity and experience. So do our literature, our theater, our paintings and our sculpture. Taken together with our holidays and our manners, the arts form a culture that embodies our understanding of life.

That point is not lost on the Park Rangers among us, who are no longer content to sue over menorahs and such, but now regularly attack musical productions, theater offerings and literary selections in public schools and elsewhere. Credit them with consistency. Removing religion from public life does indeed require more than just making off with a few manger scenes. Religious elements are deeply rooted in our culture.

There is a reason for this. As we'll discuss later, the thirst for transcendence is deeply rooted in our humanity. It's natural for us to seek truth, goodness and beauty. And it's just as natural for us to want to express what we believe we've found.

Our humanity is diminished if our culture fails to reflect these impulses—especially when other human traits that are at least as divisive as religion aren't censored from the culture. Take ethnicity: Elsewhere in the world, people still slaughter each other over it at least as much as they do over religious differences. And our Constitution bars government ethnic preferences just as stringently as it does religious ones. Yet our courts are not clogged with Serbian-Americans trying to block Croatian-American festivals. Why? Because they'd be laughed out of court. It's obvious that municipal sponsorship of such things is not a foretaste of ethnic cleansing. It's just an acknowledgment of one of the many ethnic elements of culture. It should be equally obvious that when the government wants to do precisely the same thing for the religious aspects of culture, it's not another Saint Bartholomew's Night. Stealing Easter and leaving behind "Special Bunny Day" isn't just tasteless, it's dishonest. It lies to us about who we really are.

But surely allowing believers to participate in the culture doesn't mean we also have to put up with their divisive and embarrassing preaching, does it? In public? Isn't that taking things just a little too far? These are good questions for Governor Winthrop of the Massachusetts Bay Colony, whom we'll meet in the next chapter.

FOUR

What about Prosleytizing?

Reflections on the Puritans' paranoia about dissent

Of course there were dissidents—there always are. And of course they wanted to argue—they always do. That's normal. Governor Winthrop, though, didn't look at it that way. All he could see was his good Puritans being preyed on by proselytizers. Worse yet, some were actually being converted. He would have to put a stop to it; he would have to banish the dissidents from the colony.

But the dissidents just kept coming. Winthrop had barely succeeded in banishing the first wave of them when another wave was upon him. After he had banished that wave, some of the exiled dissidents came back. And a third, larger wave would soon start to build.

There are still those among us who want to put a stop to the proselytism. Some worry about people being led into error, others about divisiveness. Still others just find it all vaguely distasteful and offensive. We may have to put up with different religions, and even with their cultural efforts, Park Rangers say, but wouldn't it all be more peaceful if we just kept a lid on all this competing proselytism? Sure, say the Pilgrims, provided that you restrict only the false religions.

How to answer them? Reflecting on the colonial dissidents and their feistiness helps us see. We'll look at the issue from both sides. We'll consider how well repressing dissidents really works (and why), and we'll touch on the ethics of proselytism, as we begin to inquire into a more fundamental question: Where does the freedom to preach—and freedom of religion in general—come from in the first place?

A Tarnished City upon a Hill

This story begins not in Plymouth but in the other, larger settlement in Massachusetts, the Bay Colony, which was centered in Boston. There, Puritans of the nonseparatist sort were determined to build a shining "City upon a Hill" in the colony they had founded in 1630. They had a somewhat different vision from Plymouth. They planned on someday returning in triumph to an England that had been so edified by their example that it had repented and become Puritan. For that vision to succeed, the colonists had to maintain the utmost purity themselves. There could be neither heretics nor unpunished sinners in Massachusetts Bay.

They were led by a forty-two-year-old lawyer and lord-of-the-manor from Lincolnshire named John Winthrop. He was a Puritan's Puritan. In a sermon delivered to his followers before they landed in Massachusetts, Winthrop warned that God would not "bear with such failings at our hands as He doth from those among whom we have lived." No, God would hold them to a higher standard than England. God had made a special covenant with them and would insist that it be "strictly observed in every article." If they strayed, God would "surely break out in wrath" to "make us know the price of the breach of such a Covenant." They were a new chosen people, their voyage a new exodus, and their colony a new promised land.

Their laws were uncompromising. Besides famously requiring adulterers to wear a scarlet A, they required gluttons to wear a G, drunks to wear a D and so on. (Had they added an E, the various sinners could have teamed up to spell "egad.") Despite what Nathanael Hawthorne tried to portray, it seems that Hester Prynne got off pretty easy—the preferred method for imposing these letters was not sewing them to one's garments, but branding them on one's skin. Early laws prescribe the manner and placement of brands, from the hands and the necks, where they might easily be hidden by collars and sleeves, to directly on the cheeks for some repeat offenders.

Needless to say, the colony tolerated no dissent. It prescribed the death penalty for some offenses, including blasphemy and being a persistent Jesuit. Lesser dissidents would be dealt with, at least initially, by banishment.

The colony was blessed with many of these. They were, as dissidents usually are, a colorful bunch.

A Cranky Genius

The most famous dissident was a young and irrepressibly cranky Cambridge divinity student named Roger Williams. A born gadfly, Williams combined an engaging personality and a fine mind with too much energy and a maddeningly fastidious faith.

Williams was a problem child from the beginning. The twenty-eight-year-old arrived in Massachusetts Bay in February 1631 and immediately caused a stir in the brand-new colony. He was offered, and promptly rejected, the prestigious position of teacher of the Boston church. Because its members had never formally renounced the Church of England, Williams said, the Boston church wasn't fit to be a church of the pure. He could not possibly be in communion with it. So he promptly left for the Bay Colony's outpost of Salem in hopes of further purifying the church there. When that didn't work, Williams left again, this time to join the separatist Pilgrims in Plymouth. But eventually even the separatists proved insufficiently separate for Williams, so he separated from them and returned to the Bay Colony.

There, Williams was in and out of trouble with the government for years. He preached against both the church and the state. He called the king a liar, for example, for purporting to grant the colony the land on which it stood. That land, Williams observed, was not the king's to give but belonged to the Indians. He added that the king was a blasphemer for referring to Europe as "the Christian World," when it manifestly wasn't Christian at all. Indeed, he said, the Church of England was actually anti-Christian.

Most tellingly, he argued that civil magistrates had no authority over purely religious matters. God, he said, wanted religious duties to be voluntarily shouldered and not coerced. And that meant people had to be free *not* to shoulder them as well. The only way to ensure that people could authentically embrace the truth was to recognize their corresponding right to reject it and embrace something else instead. As he would later sum it up, "it is the will and command of God" for "permission of the most paganish, Jewish, Turkish, or antichristian consciences and worships, [to] be granted to all men in all nations and countries." Williams might not be in communion with them; they might be grievously punished in the hereafter; but in the here-and-now people couldn't be coerced in their belief or practice.

Governor Winthrop, who was generally perplexed with Williams anyway, reacted to this last pronouncement with abject horror. Why, that would mean, Winthrop wrote, that "the magistrate might not punish the breach of the Sabbath." It would also mean that the capital offense of blasphemy would go unpunished by the state, as would idolatry. For that matter, a "church might run into heresy...and yet the civil magistrate could not intermeddle." Shocking.

The Gospel According to Roger

Let's pause for a moment to compare Williams and Winthrop. Each believed in a unique truth. Each thought he was right and the other was wrong. And each was in the proselytism business. Winthrop was trying to convert the reprobate among the Bay Colonists, who were all legally required to attend his established churches. He was also trying to convert all of England. For his part, Roger Williams was trying to convert anyone and everyone, seemingly at every moment.

But each took a sharply different approach to proselytism. To Winthrop, things couldn't be clearer. Williams was doing the unthinkable and trying to win converts to error from among the true-believing Bay Colonists. He had to be stopped at all costs and the law was the most effective weapon at hand. Nobody had the right to preach an erroneous religion, regardless of what his conscience said. A conscience that commanded someone to preach falsely was just another disorder that the godly had to remedy. And if coercion was the most effective medicine, then coercion it would be. The truth justified restricting freedom.

Williams took the opposite tack. He, too, believed in the unique truth of his vision. He was no relativist. For him, Anglicanism, Bay Colony Puritanism and his own faith were not just different paths up the same Protestant mountain. No, he was right, the others were wrong, and he would do his indefatigable best to convince them of that fact. He would argue and debate, preach, ridicule and denounce—anything he could think of to persuade them. Persuasion, though, was the limit. At the end of the day, if he failed to convince them, he wouldn't resort to coercion; that itself would violate God's command. Their mistaken consciences had to be respected. They were wrong but they had the right to be wrong.

Granted, Williams was exasperating. (We all know the type.) Nevertheless, he was on to something very big. He believed in the truth but he wasn't a Pilgrim; he believed in freedom but was no Park Ranger. He was convinced that the truth itself guaranteed freedom—while Winthrop insisted, with most everyone else in the seventeenth century, that the truth limited freedom.

It was a magnificent insight, one that was far ahead of its time, that if people are to be free to embrace the truth, they require freedom to obey their consciences even when they're mistaken. So the same freedom of conscience that gave Williams the freedom to preach gave his listeners the freedom to judge for themselves the truth or falsity of his preaching. He could preach according to his conscience; they could accept or reject it according to theirs. Persuasion, therefore, and not coercion, was the only morally acceptable form of proselytism.

Williams was right. Unfortunately he based his *argument* for his insight on a premise that not everyone could grant, namely that God's will was to give liberty of conscience to all. Had he based his argument instead not on who God is, but on who we are, he could have saved us a century or so of feeling our way forward. Like a student taking a geometry test, therefore, Williams gets only partial credit, because although he got the answer right, he got the proof wrong.

Williams' long-running confrontation with Winthrop is instructive on a more pragmatic count as well. Let's return to our story.

Trying to Banish Dissent

By 1635, Winthrop had decided to increase the pressure on Williams. First, he arranged for several clergymen to gang up with the magistrates in an attempt to silence him.

It backfired. Williams promptly denounced the conspirators' churches as no longer pure (a potent insult in a Puritan colony), and demanded that the Salem church break communion with them. That was the last straw for the authorities. Much as you couldn't separate from the separatists in Plymouth, you couldn't be purer than the Puritans in Massachusetts Bay. Williams was summoned before the General Court and banished in October 1635.

That also backfired. The court gave him until spring to leave—provided that he didn't seek "to draw others to his opinions." Of course he did precisely that, gathering about twenty followers and laying plans for a separate, truly pure settlement.

When the authorities found out, they decided to crack down even harder. If Williams wouldn't go away quietly, they would banish him immediately, and not just from the colony but from the continent. They would forcibly deport him to England.

But that backfired, too. Williams and his followers got wind of the plot. They fled, purchased land from the Narragansett tribe and established a rump settlement, which they named Providence, in what would later become Rhode Island. Now, the last thing the Bay Colonists wanted was a rival settlement preaching a rival truth on their borders. But that is precisely what their repression of Williams' preaching had created. If they had simply left him alone to rail against them, he would have remained just a cranky nuisance in their colony. Now he had his own settlement, which he could use to gather even more dissidents.

Faced with the reality of Williams' settlement, the Bay Colonists did what seemed to them the only sensible thing to do. They persecuted it. They challenged its legality under

English law in an attempt to have it dismantled. They excluded it from the mutual defense pact of all the other Puritan colonies in the hopes that the Indians would do it in. Eventually, they even considered invading it themselves.

All of which backfired. It made Williams and his followers more convinced than ever that the Bay Colony deserved their denunciations. They began sending out missionaries.

Winthrop's Folly

The insight here is in the category of mistakes-not-to-make. It's something we might call Winthrop's Folly—the notion that religious divisiveness is minimized by repressing proselytism in public. The lesson that Winthrop should have learned, but never did, was that dissent, and therefore proselytism and conversion, are functions of conscience. So you can harass dissidents and persecute them; you can drive proselytism underground for a time. But you can't ever really silence it. Conscience is far too stubborn. And driving it underground increases its divisiveness when it resurfaces.

Of Nimble Wits and Weak Parts

Meanwhile, back in Boston, Governor Winthrop thought he'd quelled dissent. But of course he hadn't. The next wave, led by Anne Hutchinson, was soon upon him. And his mistaken assumptions in dealing with it highlight the limitations of the state in matters of religious truth.

Hutchinson was an attractive, middle-aged, well-to-do force of nature. Winthrop called her "a woman of a haughty and fierce carriage," with a "nimble wit and active spirit." (She was married, he added, to "a man of very mild temper and weak parts.")

With weak-parted husband and children in tow, Hutchinson had followed her favorite Puritan preacher from England into exile in the Bay Colony. She arrived in Boston in 1634 and moved into a large house across the street from Governor Winthrop. Soon she was using it to host weekly gatherings in which she plunged headlong into the religious issues of the day. Hutchinson was quickly gathering about her a growing circle of women, which was considered barely acceptable—as well as a growing circle of men, which was not. Before long, the crowds were spilling out of the house, with some people having to stand outside and lean in the open windows.

Hutchinson's views were at least as unorthodox as Roger Williams' were, though in a different way. Where Williams accepted the basic Puritan premise but took it to extremes, Hutchinson implicitly disputed that premise. For her there were two kinds of Christians: those who thought their upright lives were evidence of their inward spiritual transformation, and those who just knew they had truly been chosen by God regardless of how they lived their lives. The first were living under a "covenant of works," she said, the second under a superior "covenant of grace."

That was, to put it mildly, divisive. And peering across the street, the governor was not amused. It "began to be [as] common here," Winthrop wrote, to distinguish between people according to Hutchinson's categories as it was to distinguish "in other countries between Protestants and papists." So Hutchinson found herself before the General Court in November 1637, charged with holding "disorderly meetings" in her home, "tending to the subversion of the Christian faith," and dishonoring the authorities. She was, of course, convicted and exiled, together with her family and her followers. The court decided she would be "banished out of our liberties" (some liberties!) due to the "troublesomeness of her spirit and the danger of her course" to the welfare of the community. (This band of exiles, too, headed for Rhode Island, where they founded Portsmouth and provided reinforcements to a beleaguered if feisty Roger Williams.)

It is instructive to note *how* Anne Hutchinson was convicted.

Trying Again to Banish Dissent

Hutchinson's trial began with "the court" (read: "Governor Winthrop") demanding to know whether she "countenanced" the "seditious practices" of her followers who were agitating the colony. She answered this question with a telling question of her own: were they examining her on a "point of conscience"? The court, in true Puritan fashion, replied, "No, your conscience you may keep to your self." She was being examined, Winthrop said, "not for your conscience, but for your practice." In other words, she could think whatever she wanted; she just couldn't tell anybody.

Especially about her revelations. It seems that while she was still in England, Hutchinson had been told by God that she would be persecuted in Massachusetts, but would be delivered and the colony itself brought to ruin. This was too much for the governor to bear. Hutchinson was, Winthrop said, following "such a rule as cannot stand with the peace of any State." He reasoned that "such bottomlesse revelations...If they be allowed in one thing, must be admitted a rule in all things." That is, if the court let her go, it would be admitting that her revelations must be true—and so would be stuck with whatever she might dream up next.

That, of course, didn't really follow at all. It made sense to Winthrop only because of his unquestioned assumption that no government could tolerate heresy. He simply lacked the imagination of a Roger Williams; it was unthinkable for Winthrop to say, as Williams would, that Hutchinson's revelations were nonsense, but she could go on preaching them if her conscience told her to. And everyone else would be equally free to follow her, denounce her or ignore her as their consciences told them. No, for Winthrop there were only two choices: either Hutchinson was a true prophet of God or the government must do its best to silence her.

Still Trying to Banish Dissent

The lesson for our Pilgrims and Park Rangers is that the government does not endorse every message it permits, nor may it censor religious messages it disapproves. It is not our nanny; it is not responsible for what we are permitted to hear.

This may sound obvious. And indeed it is—in every area except religion. Among bureaucrats, and even some lower courts, Winthrop's notion is still alive and unfortunately well.

Contemporary Pilgrims continue trying to use the law to restrict recruiting for religions they believe to be false. A variety of faiths have faced their disapproval.

The best example is Los Angeles, where indignant airport commissioners prevented Jews for Jesus from preaching in airport terminals. Their tolerance for public preaching was so low they actually passed a resolution banning all "First Amendment activities" in the airport, a phrasing that didn't go over particularly well with the Supreme Court. The Court has likewise had to vindicate the right to preach publicly for Jehovah's Witnesses, Hare Krishnas and the Unification Church.

There are also peculiar sorts of part-time Pilgrims who think preaching is expendable enough that they can freely ban it on certain subjects. The Clinton administration, for instance, felt free to order military chaplains not to preach against Clinton's veto of a ban on partial-birth abortion. (A Becket Fund lawsuit resulted in a scathing opinion from a federal district court striking down the order.) Others threaten hate-speech prosecutions of those who preach the traditional moral line on gay sex. In short, these part-time Pilgrims have a specific point of view on a certain subject that they think is so obviously true that it justifies censoring religious dissent on it. They're not Pilgrims most of the time, just when their favorite issues are in play.

Many Park Rangers agree with the Pilgrims. They, too, think that nobody should be allowed to recruit for a false religion—it's just that they think all religion is false. So they attempt to discourage religious recruiting in public as much as they can. Other Park Rangers are (at least privately) kinder toward faith. They don't necessarily think it's false. But they nevertheless agree it should be discouraged in public. Why? Because it's divisive. City officials in Mishawaka, Indiana, are a good example. They prohibited a resident from placing a sign with a religious message on his front lawn. Never mind that he and his neighbors had been putting up political signs in their yards for years; religion was presumably more divisive than politics.

And, in fairness, sometimes it has been. So has sex. And ethnicity. And all the other deeply human attachments that are so close to the core of who we are. The question is not how to try to erase those aspects of our humanity. The question is how to live with disagreements over them. Part of the answer, again, is respect for people's duty to follow their consciences even when we are sure they are mistaken. Another part is for the state to recognize its limits and not try to enforce religious truth.

This is not because there is no such thing as religious truth. (Most of us are convinced there is.) Nor is it because the state can never know what that is. (Both Israel and the Vatican City State certainly think they know, and England claims to think so.) It is because the state may not coerce the consciences of its citizens, even if it really does know the truth.

The Quaker Persecutions Pose the Big Question

The Puritans thought they finally had everything under control. Roger Williams and Anne Hutchinson were both off in exile in Rhode Island, and the Puritans even had hopes that they could pressure that whole scandalous settlement into folding. At last things seemed to be settling down.

Then the Quakers appeared on the horizon. And the Bay Colony began to contemplate a different sort of dissident—one determined to speak the truth to it no matter what. Faced with this prospect, the Puritans soon lost what little patience they had ever had for heretics. In fact, they began to grow positively cruel.

The story of their legalized cruelty and of the Quakers' heroism in the face of it leads us to begin reflecting on a crucial question: Where does the freedom to preach—and by extension, religious liberty itself—come from? Is it a creature of the state, or do its origins lie elsewhere?

The Inner Light

The Quakers, or the Society of Friends, emerged in England in 1652, as the Reformation continued to fracture. More radical than the Puritans, Quakers rejected sacraments, ordained clergy and church structure. They relied instead on the leading of the

Inner Light, the internal promptings that they believed were nothing less than the voice of God. The Inner Light was thus even more authoritative than conscience. And it could be gloriously unpredictable. It led not only to a personal love of God, but sometimes to prophetic sorts of action. The Inner Light had even been known on occasion to lead Quakers to turn up at Anglican services naked.

Needless to say, Massachusetts Bay wanted no part of them. So, in October 1656, the General Court passed a law forbidding Quakers from coming into the colony and prescribing flogging for any who persisted.

To the amazement of the Bay Colonists, however, the Quakers simply refused to obey this law. Banished Quakers often returned, sometimes repeatedly, to preach and, if necessary, be flogged. So, the next year, the Bay Colony passed more laws. A male Quaker who returned would "for the first offense have one of his ears cut off." For a second offense he would "have his other ear cut off." A Quaker woman would only be "severely whipped" for the first or second offense. But for a third offense both men and women would be treated alike. They would "have their tongues bored through with a hot iron."

That didn't deter them, either. Christopher Holder, John Copeland and John Rous, for example, insisted on returning from exile to preach. So, on July 17, 1658, in a prison cell in Boston, each lost his right ear.

Surely that would put a stop to them. But no, the Quakers still came back to preach against a government that was looking ever more deserving of their condemnation. The Bay Colony responded by further digging in its heels. Three months later, in October 1658, the General Court passed yet another law. It provided that any outsider found guilty of being a Quaker "shall be sentenced to banishment upon pain of death."

Why? The anti-Quaker laws were explicit about their purpose: to prevent Quakers from "seeking to turn the People from the Faith, and gain Proselites." The death penalty for returning Quakers was added when, "notwithstanding all former laws," Quakers continued to spread their ideas and many of the colonists were being "infected" with them. They had to be stopped at all costs, even death.

But the Inner Light would not be shuttered. So, undeterred, the Quakers continued to return to the Bay Colony. One of the most adamant was Anne Hutchinson's friend and early follower, Mary Dyer.

Enter (Briefly) Mary Dyer

Mary Dyer was, Governor Winthrop had thought, "a very proper and comely young woman." It turned out she was very much a free spirit besides. She went back to the Bay Colony repeatedly to preach about the Inner Light and to denounce the legalized persecution of her fellow Quakers, to "try the bloody law," as she put it. She went back four times, in fact (not counting the two trips she took to preach in the Puritan colony of New Haven).

So, on June 1, 1660, following her fourth arrest, she was solemnly hanged on Boston Common.

She had, the good magistrates said, been warned. The previous October, when she had been arrested for the third time, had she not witnessed two other Quakers, William Robinson and Marmaduke Stevenson, hang for the same offence? And hadn't the magistrates then formally sentenced her to death as well, even putting a noose about her neck before mercifully releasing her and expelling her one final time? But she had returned yet again and was obviously unrepentant. So the fault was hers, they said, as they legally killed her for preaching in Massachusetts.

The king was disturbed by news of Mary Dyer's hanging. He ordered the executions stopped and commanded that imprisoned Quakers be transferred to London instead of tried in the colony. The Bay Colony authorities complied with the king's order, but only reluctantly. And only partially. They did stop executing people. (News of the king's order arrived just in time to save the lives of a number of Quakers who were then in prison, but too late for William Leddra, who had been executed just days before.) But in 1661 they replaced the death penalty with a new law. It provided that if any "wandering" Quaker appeared in the colony, "he or shee" was to be "stripped naked from the middle upwards, and tyed to a Cart's tail, and whipped through the Town." Upon reaching the town limits, the victim was to be handed over to the next town's authorities, who would repeat the process. This torture would continue in each successive town until the unfortunate Quaker had been beaten and dragged to the borders of the Bay Colony itself.

Why did the Puritans do all this? In a stunning bit of doublespeak, the General Court later said that it was actually for "liberty of conscience" that it had been "necessitated to make more severe laws to prevent the violent and impetuous intrusions of the Quakers." They meant, of course, for the "liberty" of *their* consciences. The Quakers' consciences couldn't have any liberty because the Quakers' consciences were by definition wrong.

That, in a sentence, was the root of the Puritans' problem: they thought it was only a conscience that agreed with theirs that was entitled to freedom of expression. Everybody else's could be legally restricted.

But What About the Law?

Note that both sides of the double standard—the Puritans' privileges and the Quakers' persecutions—were completely legal. The legislature had passed both into law. Granted, the Bay Colony authorities were as monstrous as the Quakers were heroic. Still, wasn't their law, as abhorrent as it was, nevertheless the law? Where did the Quakers get off breaking it?

Or, put differently: Didn't Mary Dyer have it coming? After all, the proper authorities in the colony had duly enacted the law under which she was executed. She had notice of that law. She deliberately broke it. And she was properly tried and found guilty. So why didn't Mary Dyer deserve to hang?

Because executing anyone for his or her religious expression is immoral. Duly enacted, schmuly enacted. It's wrong. And if the law says otherwise, then the law is wrong. But why?

Maybe the problem was with *executing* her. Maybe if they'd done something less, there wouldn't have been a problem. What about Holder, Copeland and Rous, the three Quakers who only had their ears cut off—perfectly lawfully—for insisting on preaching illegally in the colony. Is there anything wrong with that? Again, the law was duly enacted and they knew they were breaking it and what the penalty was. Why shouldn't they—and Mary Dyer—at least lose their ears or have their tongues bored through with a hot iron?

Because that, too, is immoral. Law or no law, it's wrong to mutilate someone for preaching. Why, though? Perhaps because maiming is always wrong? Well, then, what of the "cart's tail law," which, you'll recall, required a Quaker to be "stripped naked from the middle upwards, and tyed to a Cart's tail, and whipped" through one town after another until he or she was expelled from the Bay Colony? No lasting injuries. What if they'd only done that to Mary Dyer?

It would still be outrageous.

And if they'd merely applied the original law and simply flogged her for preaching against the established religion and trying to make converts from it?

Same thing.

But if you can't do any of those things, then how can you legally banish her—or Williams or Hutchinson? After all, these various penalties were just designed to enforce banishment. The Puritans had gone to great lengths and taken extraordinary risks to establish a colony of their choosing. Couldn't they maintain its distinctive character by kicking out those they found undesirable?

Yes and no. As a general matter, the colony was certainly free to expel criminals. But it was not free to criminalize anything and everything in the first place. It could banish undesirables, but not for just any reason. Moreover, it couldn't enforce even a legitimate banishment with any and all penalties no matter how cruel or barbaric.

Well, if not, why not? The reason can't be because these things are unconstitutional; they weren't unconstitutional then—there wasn't a constitution. And it can't be because they are illegal; they were perfectly legal then. There was even a law that *required* them.

It's because there are moral limits on the government's power, limits that follow from who we are. We call them "rights." And they're valid always and everywhere—even without a law that recognizes them, and even despite a law that attempts to override them.

It would be over a century before the idea of rights would catch on in America. And even when it did, it was still problematic. It wasn't always well thought-through. (If rights follow from who we are, who are we? And how do you know?) And the rights that were recognized were almost immediately compromised. But the advent of rights theory would be a tremendous step forward nevertheless. We'll tell those stories and take up those questions later. In the meantime there were important intermediate advances, the ideas of conscientious objection and tolerance, which we'll look at in the next two chapters.

Though the early Quakers and other dissidents didn't know it, help was on the way. Slowly. Painfully slowly. As we'll soon discover, the Quakers had more to suffer—and more insights to share—before even a semblance of religious liberty would arrive.

FIVE

Heavens No, We Won't Go

*Reflections on how the Quakers
invented conscientious objection*

They weren't just heretics; they were outlaws. And it wasn't just their insistence on preaching and it wasn't just in Massachusetts Bay. The Quakers' refusal to swear oaths or serve in the military was illegal just about everywhere. In the eyes of the authorities, it was bad enough that they were unorthodox; now they were refusing to pull their weight and swear their loyalty besides. They would have to be made to obey. They would swear and they would serve—or they would suffer for it.

They chose, of course, to suffer for it. But they won in the end.

In fact, they won so completely and accommodations for religious scruples about oath-taking and military service are now so commonplace that it's easy to forget the story of how they came to be. And this, in turn, obscures the larger lesson that the Quakers and their gentle stubbornness teach: that religious freedom includes the freedom to be different. Not just the freedom to think differently from the powers-that-be. Nor just the freedom to try to persuade others to think differently. Nor even just the freedom to celebrate those different ideas publicly. No, religious freedom includes the freedom to *be* different, to organize one's entire life around those ideas. To behave, in other words, as if the truths we believe might actually be true.

What happens, though, when conscience forbids doing something that the law requires, or conversely, requires doing something that the law forbids? Does conscience trump law, and if it does, how can it get away with it? Isn't that just garden-variety lawlessness?

Let's see.

I Couldn't Swear to It

The Quakers' refusal to swear oaths seems, to current sensibilities, rather quaint—just the sort of low-impact religious exercise we like to make a big show of accommodating. But the seventeenth and eighteenth centuries, for all their faults, weren't so jaded. For people then, refusal to take an oath was telling. Far from a mere formality, an oath solemnly bound a person before God, either to tell the truth or to behave in a certain way. So a foresworn oath represented not just some calculated risk of a perjury prosecution, but a fearsome prospect of eternal damnation. People didn't take—or refuse—oaths lightly. (Thomas More, for one, went to his death for refusing to swear an oath he didn't believe.) In essence, oaths were thought to be the only real guarantee of proper behavior when no one was looking. Refusing to swear them was tantamount to refusing to be a member of society.

The Quakers, though, were adamant: To take an oath would be to sin. All oaths, they believed, had been forbidden by Jesus himself. So they couldn't take any. Period. They would be happy to affirm what was true, but they couldn't swear to it.

In the seventeenth century, however, you couldn't just politely decline an oath, or cheerfully offer to "affirm" instead. There were major consequences to either course of action. In 1659 Plymouth there were twelve convictions for refusal to take the oath of allegiance to England and the colony. Maryland had a more straightforward approach: they simply threw offending Quakers directly in jail. Other colonies did the same. Virginia's governor implemented the Act for Suppressing Quakers, which levied heavy fines on a variety of Quaker activities. A Quaker named Thomas Jordan was arrested at a meeting and taken to court, where authorities attempted to administer an oath. When he refused, he was imprisoned for ten months and ten of his cattle were confiscated. His wife was later imprisoned alongside him. Even normally tolerant North Carolina, where many Quakers made their home, forced all Quakers out of public office. Parliament had enacted an oath requirement, and Quakers found they could not serve both their government and their own consciences. Oaths were mandatory and refusing them was a crime.

There were a few early exceptions—Rhode Island and Quaker-settled Pennsylvania stand out. For the most part, though, the Quakers' refusal to swear oaths was met with unremitting hostility up to the revolutionary period. And the Revolutionary War itself made things particularly difficult. After all, if Quakers wouldn't swear their loyalty, how could you tell whose side they were on?

In 1776, the Continental Congress passed an act requiring an oath of allegiance of any man who was not clearly a patriot; anyone who refused would be considered an enemy. Some states went even further: Virginia declared that any man who would not take the oath would not be permitted to buy land or sue for debts, and his hunting rifle would be confiscated. The following year, the commonwealth doubled the taxes of anyone who refused the oath. Massachusetts cut off all supplies to Nantucket Island, a Quaker stronghold, and many residents came close to starvation.

But the Quakers simply wouldn't budge. And, as a result, something between tolerance and admiration began to take root. In 1777, for example, authorities in revolutionary Philadelphia had rounded up forty prominent citizens and required them to swear an oath of allegiance to the colonies, or else be banished. Nearly half were Quakers who had refused the oath on principle and so were sent off to Virginia in the middle of the Pennsylvania winter. But General Washington heard of their predicament and intervened, allowing the Quakers to return.

This was neither Washington's first, nor his last, encounter with the Quakers. More than twenty years earlier, in 1756 Virginia, then-Colonel George Washington had released a number of Quakers who had been arrested for refusing service in his militia unit. And later in life he answered with more mature reflection the letters that Quakers wrote to him as president: "I assure you very especially that in my opinion the conscientious scruples of all men should be treated with great delicacy and tenderness; and it is my wish and desire that the laws may always be extensively accommodated to them as a due regard to the protection and essential interest of the nation may justify."

In fact, accommodation of the Quakers' refusal of oaths was beginning to grow generally. Faced with the Quakers' insistent objections, the authorities were waking up to the fact that people who preferred being fined to violating their consciences were likely to be very trustworthy even without an oath. There was just not much point in trying to get blood from this particular turnip. By 1780, it seemed that everybody was in the accommodation business. The newly free states were writing their constitutions, and every state that wrote in an oath of office during this time period allowed an affirmation as a substitute. (Provided, of course, that you affirmed you were a Christian along the way. We had come far—but we still had a long way to go.)

By the time the federal Constitution was written in 1787, the idea of accommodating Quakers was well established. Accordingly, the framers included two such provisions in the Constitution itself: Article II specifies that the presidential oath of office may be taken either by swearing *or by affirming.* Article IV allows the same substitution for the congressional oath of office. So, in a remarkable turnabout, the society that had seen Quakers executed a century before was now making accommodations in case one of them should ever be elected president.

Remarkable as it was, though, it was still only an example of something we might call the "easy accommodation." It's the type of accommodation that is cost-effective, that makes practical sense. The Quakers were trustworthy folk and were willing to substitute something else—an affirmation—that served the same purpose as an oath anyway. It was less trouble making the adjustment that their consciences required than it was prosecuting them. But what about the difficult accommodation, the one that doesn't seem cost-effective at all, the one that makes sense only if we factor in a high value for conscience itself? What about, say, pacifism in time of war?

Turning the Other Cheek...and the Other Cheek...and...

While the oath saga was unfolding, a similar story was playing itself out over compulsory military service. Military service was literally a life–and-death matter to the colonies. That was all the more true since no colony had a standing army. Instead, each depended entirely on a citizen militia—the military equivalent of a volunteer fire department—that included every able-bodied adult male. Local skirmishes were not uncommon and in small towns with modest populations, even a few pacifists refusing to fight could make a significant difference.

But to the Quakers, bearing arms was a sin. Jesus, they pointed out, had said in the Sermon on the Mount to turn the other cheek. On their reading of that, military service was out of the question. So no matter how pressing the need, they wouldn't bear arms, ever. The powers-that-be were beside themselves.

By 1658, pacifists were already in trouble in the colonies. That year, a Maryland Quaker refused to join the militia and suffered a beating from the sheriff, who threatened to "split [his] brains." An elderly Quaker had much of his life savings confiscated for refusing to join; another impoverished Quaker had to sell his only real asset—his cow—when punished with a heavy fine. (And when the authorities got wind of the sale, they seized both the fine and the man's meager profits.)

Things got worse, and not just in Maryland. Virginia levied a hefty fine, one hundred pounds of tobacco, on anyone who wouldn't serve in the militia. Massachusetts Bay passed a law disenfranchising anyone who opposed military service, although, as we've seen, Quakers there had bigger problems.

There were two early—temporary—exceptions for religious conscientious objectors. Pennsylvania and Rhode Island both enacted (and later revoked) laws protecting them. In 1673, Rhode Island provided for alternative service: caring for "weak and aged impotent persons, women and children, goods and cattle." In 1677, though, during a local war with the Wampanoag tribe, a successor government of the colony revoked the exemption and levied fines for refusal to serve. Pennsylvania at first went far beyond accommodation. The Quaker-settled colony actually refused to form a militia at all. But after the beginning of the French and Indian War (and after considerable ire from the Crown), the colony gave in and created a strictly voluntary militia. By the time the Revolutionary War was in full swing, though, Pennsylvania had made a complete reversal: it resorted to conscription of every able-bodied white male between 18 and 53. And a heavy fine awaited anyone who refused to serve. In short, at one point or another, all colonies required service in the militia and backed up that requirement with stiff penalties.

It didn't always have to be service in person, though. Many colonies allowed people to hire a substitute or pay a substantial fine and stay home. This did nothing, however, to assuage the Quakers' consciences. They saw these so-called "allowances" for what they were—buyouts for landowners, not accommodations for conscientious objectors. So most refused them. If an action is morally wrong, they asked, is it any better to hire somebody else to do it for you? Many Quakers refused even to pay the fines levied against them for refusing to serve. They saw the fines as merely disguised allowances, with the money going to pay soldiers or buy weapons.

They were heroic; they were incorrigible. They were both. They wouldn't fight; they wouldn't pay someone else to fight for them; they wouldn't even pay their fines. And they insisted that all the trouble they were causing was morally required. What to do with such people?

Most colonies began to seize their property—even though it was often worth much more than the fines that the seizures were supposed to cover. The Quakers, though, were immovable. Losing their property or even going to jail was certainly unpleasant, but it didn't change what their consciences required. Something was going to have to give.

The Quakers got their first big break in 1775, when they persuaded the Continental Congress to exempt religious CO's from service (though the exemption was not always observed in practice—one North Carolina Quaker was even whipped with a cat-o'-nine-tails for refusal to serve). And during the revolutionary period, four states—Delaware, New York, New Hampshire and Pennsylvania (again)—wrote religion-based CO exemptions into their new state constitutions. Later, after independence, when the Bill of Rights was being debated in the U.S. Congress, James Madison proposed making religiously based conscientious objection a federal constitutional right. He suggested that what would later become the Second Amendment guarantee not only a right to bear arms but also that "no person religiously scrupulous of bearing arms shall be compelled to render military service in person." Congress declined. Still, the idea of accommodation was continuing to make headway—during ratification, two new states, North Carolina and Virginia, joined Rhode Island, and Pennsylvania in asking for an amendment protecting religious conscientious objection.

The trend continued. The Civil War brought the United States its first national draft, and more protests from Quakers on both sides. In North Carolina, twelve Quakers who refused to serve were imprisoned, tied up and beaten. Military officials singled out Seth Laughlin, a recent Quaker convert, for special attention. He was deprived of sleep, beaten daily, and literally hung from his thumbs. When that didn't work, he was court-martialed and sentenced to death. Facing his firing squad, he asked for permission to pray. It was granted, the officials believing he wished to pray for himself. Instead, he prayed for them and quoted Jesus' prayer from the cross: "Father, forgive them, for they know not what they do." The firing squad knew when they'd been beaten and dropped their weapons.

Change in the North was effected more politically. Congress's conscription bill had no conscientious objector exemptions, only a $300 fine for those who refused to serve. So the Quakers set to work petitioning President Lincoln for an exemption. They finally got what they wanted. The new CO exemption provided members of the peace churches with the option of working in hospitals or aiding former slaves, and if they chose to pay the fine instead, that money would go to hospitals and former slaves as well. And with that, the Quakers won. Their stubborn adherence to their consciences had created a new category of national service in time of war.

The CO movement was now irreversible. During World War I, the federal government again instituted alternative service for religious noncombatants, most of whom ended up working in hospitals. The same was true in World War II. And during the Vietnam War, the Supreme Court stretched the CO exemption to include those with beliefs that are "sincere and meaningful" and "occup[y] a place...parallel to that filled by the orthodox belief in God." So freedom of conscience was broadened; the exemption that used to be limited to religiously based objectors now applied to all CO's.

But still only to CO's. *Conscientious* objectors don't have to serve in combat. Other objectors—those who think that war is unwise or too expensive, for example—still do. Now, why should this be? Why accommodate *conscientious* objectors and not all the other sorts of objectors? For that matter, why make difficult accommodations for conscientious objectors at all? This is the larger lesson in the Quakers' victory.

Learning from Yossarian

Yossarian in Joseph Heller's classic novel, *Catch-22*, makes the point well. Yossarian doesn't want to fly combat missions. Why? Because, he says, the enemy is "trying to kill me." "They're trying to kill everybody," his commander responds. "What difference does that make?" Yossarian replies. He has a point, of sorts. His best chance at self-preservation is to stay on the ground. By what right can the state force him to risk his life and fly? His commander, of course, has a point, too—the same point the early colonists had. It's generally thought that a war that threatens the state threatens everyone in it, and the state can justly conscript everyone to defend it. So Yossarian has to fly despite his perfectly rational misgivings.

But the state isn't really conscripting everyone; it's excusing conscientious objectors. Had Yossarian said that he couldn't fly combat missions because killing the enemy was morally wrong, he could have been a medic instead of a bomber pilot. Why?

Why is *conscientious* objection to killing better than garden-variety fear of being killed? What's the difference?

Conscientious objectors enjoy a preferred place in our legal regime because their refusal to fight is not based on cowardice (plenty of CO's have lost their lives serving as medics; two have even won the Medal of Honor), or on mere intransigence, but on obedience to their perceived moral duty. They won't fight because they may not fight. Their consciences forbid it. And we now see as a society that it's wrong to force someone to violate his or her conscience—especially in a matter as serious as taking human life. Conscientious objectors are different because conscience is different. Thanks to the Quakers, we get it.

Sort of. We get that pacifists have a right not to serve in combat. And we get that the early Quakers were the good guys in the story of how this came to be. It's the larger lesson we're still a little shaky on. Pilgrims and Park Rangers alike profess admiration for the Quakers—but also disdain for the sort of pluralism that accommodates other, less popular sorts of CO's today. The result is cognitive dissonance, as they acknowledge a right of conscientious objection to military service but deny it for things much less momentous—vaccinations, for example.

Of course, it's easy to admire the early Quakers, now that they're dead. They're not here to insist on any more points of conscience, so we don't have to put up with them. Heroes from the past can safely be placed on pedestals without fear of any present inconvenience. What's more, the Quakers' objections to bearing arms and swearing oaths are now neatly provided for in law. As we've seen, a federal statute protects CO's from combat duty and the Constitution itself provides the alternative of an "oath or affirmation." All perfectly respectable. No muss, no fuss heroes of conscience.

But what should we think of the Quakers before the exemption laws were written? Should we agree with the Bay Colony that they were criminals—who somehow later mutated into heroes only when the law recognized them? No, they were always heroes of conscience. If anything, they were more heroic when they stood firm in the face of a hostile state. Like Gandhi, who began his nonviolent campaign to oust the British from

India by breaking the tax law—making bootleg salt. And Martin Luther King Jr., who spoke for dissidents everywhere when he wrote from his cell in the Birmingham Jail, where he was being held for parading without a permit. He said that one who "breaks a law that conscience tells him is unjust" and accepts the penalty in order "to arouse the conscience of the community" does a great thing.

Well, then, what should we think of other sorts of less popular conscientious objectors today? Do you have to be long dead (and on the winning side) to be a hero of conscience? What of Orthodox Jews, who must keep the Sabbath? What of the Amish, who must shun technology; of the Plymouth Brethren, who may not serve on juries; of Jehovah's Witnesses, who may not salute the flag? What of doctors and nurses from a variety of faiths who may not assist in abortions? Unless the government decides to give them a break and make a special law to accommodate them, are they just some sort of outlaw?

No. If we're to be logically consistent, we must recognize them as conscientious objectors, too. That means we should affirmatively accommodate—or at least decline to prosecute or convict—such people every bit as much as we do CO's from military service. What's more, we should do it for the same reason: Modern CO's, like their early Quaker counterparts, don't conform because they may not conform. Their consciences will not permit it. And conscience, we have learned, is different from intransigence.

Again, there are limits. Some laws are so vital that they cannot be amended or excepted. Some practices are so dangerous that they cannot be tolerated. Sometimes, you just have to prosecute. And sometimes, people will have to suffer the consequences. By following their consciences and accepting the consequences, those people may eventually be vindicated, like the early Quakers. Or, like the would-be Islamist shoe-bomber Richard Reid, they may not be vindicated at all but rightfully punished as a menace to the community.

How to draw the line between conscience and the common good has always been a thorny question. (And it has recently become even thornier as a result of the Supreme Court's shifting interpretation of the First Amendment, which we'll get into later on.) But we must never forget the lesson that the early Quakers taught us at so high a price: Conscientious objection is a fundamental part of religious liberty. Consequently, religious practices should be prosecuted only when they pose a genuine, here-and-now danger to the community.

An Expensive Right

Yet what can accommodation of conscience possibly look like in a pluralistic society where disagreements are no longer simply between Protestants on the one hand and Quakers on the other, and are not over just one or two subjects like oaths and conscription? In postmodern America, after all, there are literally hundreds of religious traditions, which dissent from an untold number of different requirements. Perhaps accommodation is now too expensive. Perhaps we could afford a robust religious liberty when all we had to do was allow a small percentage of the citizenry exemptions from one or two requirements. But how can we possibly have virtually everyone exempt from something or other? The price may simply be too high.

These are valid questions. There are, however, at least two responses to them. First (and getting a bit ahead of ourselves), the fact that a human right may be expensive does not make it any less a human right. Second, the price of *not* recognizing broad rights of conscience may well prove to be even higher in the long run. There are really only two choices: an untidy pluralism that maximizes conscience, or a neat, orderly uniformity that minimizes it. A government that seeks to minimize the consciences of its citizens may well find itself, in a generation or two, in a predicament far worse than having too many principled people claiming too many points of conscience. It may find itself with too few principled people to sustain a society. As President Washington summarized the lesson that the early Quakers taught: It is a good thing that the law "always be extensively accommodated" to the "conscientious scruples of all" insofar as the "essential interest of the nation" may allow. That is, the law should bend over backward for people's consciences, though there are, necessarily, limits.

The Quakers and other religious minorities won over some

colonies more than others. As we will soon see, some tolerated them completely, for a time.

For a time? Why only for a time? Because being tolerated, while better than being persecuted, is nowhere near as good as having rights.

SIX

Why Tolerance Is Intolerable

Reflections on the failure of the refuge colonies

Quakers weren't the only ones getting hanged in colonial America. And Massachusetts Bay wasn't the only colony doing the hanging. Maryland, which was founded to be tolerant of Catholics, wound up executing some of them instead.

Typical. Maryland's hanging the very people it was supposed to tolerate is only the most extreme example of a failure common to all the so-called refuge colonies. Pennsylvania, which was founded by Quakers, ended up trying to conscript them, pacifism notwithstanding, into the militia. Rhode Island, which was begun almost entirely as a haven for religious minorities, was, within a generation, forbidding Jews to vote. And the Carolinas, which were a different sort of experiment in tolerance (their original constitution was drafted by the Enlightenment philosopher John Locke) flopped completely. Before long, they had reverted to garden-variety establishments of Anglicanism.

Tolerance was the best idea the early colonies had on religion. What went wrong with it? The same things that have been going wrong with it ever since: The government changes its mind, or lacks imagination, or both. The authority to choose to tolerate presumes the authority *not* to tolerate. Any government that thinks it is being generous, or shrewd, or pragmatic to put up with dissident faiths necessarily believes it has the power to persecute them if circumstances change. Tolerance, in short, is just a policy choice of the government, not a right of the people. And policy choices can be reversed.

The notion of tolerance, though, is a Rasputin of an idea. Thoroughly discredited, it refuses to die. Even today, Pilgrims and Park Rangers speak glibly of their virtuous tolerance, be it the "tolerance" of minority religions or "tolerance" of public religion in the first place. The stories of the refuge colonies demonstrate well why we should mistrust them both.

We'll begin with the story of the most spectacular failure, Maryland.

How Long Must I Put Up with You? The Maryland Story

In 1629, an English courtier named George Calvert called in a royal chit. The king owed Calvert a big favor and Calvert knew just how to take advantage of it. Some years earlier (before he was forced out of government for converting to Catholicism), Calvert had been instrumental in the marriage negotiations for then-Prince Charles. Just before taking the crown, Charles married a princess of France. Her name was Henrietta Maria and she, too, was a Catholic.

The marriage treaty guaranteed Henrietta Maria and her attendants the "free exercise" of their Catholic religion (and not just private belief in it) in a religiously tumultuous England. Calvert had an idea: Why not parlay the favor that the now-King Charles owed him into an American colony where Calvert and his fellow Catholics could have the same free exercise of their religion as Henrietta Maria now enjoyed? The king agreed and gave Calvert his colony, which was shrewdly named Maryland—in honor of both the Blessed Virgin Mary and Henrietta Maria. So far, so good.

But then Calvert died and his son, Cecil, formally received the royal charter and set about the business of governing. He promptly outlined a general "toleration" for his new colony along the lines of his father's thought. Under Calvert's toleration, "all sorts who profess *Christianity*...might be at Liberty to worship God in such manner as [is] most agreeable with their respective Judgments and Consciences." This was, for its time, generous.

But it was still in principle stingy. Even before the new

colony had any people in it, when it still existed only on paper, its tolerance was already restricted. It was limited to Christians, thus excluding, among others, Jews. The Calverts' lack of imagination points up a fundamental problem with tolerance. It is always arbitrarily limited to some favored kinds of infidels and leaves others out in the cold.

Two years later, in 1634, about two hundred people arrived in Maryland, said the first Catholic Mass in the British colonies, and began the countdown to yet another problem with tolerance. It is inherently temporary and fragile. In this case it lasted only about a decade. In the mid 1640s, Protestant colonists seized control of Maryland, arrested Catholic leaders and sent them back to England in chains. George Calvert's idealistic, if limited, vision of tolerance simply evaporated.

Fortunes changed again and in 1649 the Maryland Assembly passed its own Act of Toleration, broader than the Calverts'. Significantly, it provided that no one should be molested "for, or in respect of his or her religion nor in the *free exercise* thereof," thus introducing George Calvert's favorite phrase into the American legal lexicon. Some provisions even had a vaguely utopian flavor, including what must surely have been the first hate-speech legislation on American soil. It prescribed a stiff fine for colonists calling each other religious epithets—such as "heritick, scismatick, idolator...or any other name or terme in a reproachfull manner relating to matter of religion."

But Calvert's Maryland still had a very limited imagination. Once again, it stretched as far as all Christians, but no farther. And immediately after granting broad tolerance, and outlawing insults, it provided the death penalty for certain forms of heresy.

In 1654 the seesaw continued as a Protestant majority in the Maryland Assembly repealed the Act of Toleration. The next year, following a pitched battle, Puritan leaders condemned ten Catholics to death and succeeded in executing four of them. After further machinations, the Church of England was legally established in Maryland in 1692—ironically as a result of England's own so-called Act of Toleration (about which more later). The new, exclusively Protestant government disenfranchised

Catholics and prohibited them from worshipping publicly. For almost the next century, in a bitter irony, Catholics were an oppressed minority in a colony named in part for the Blessed Virgin Mary.

The lesson is simple. Tolerance based solely on the government's benevolence lasts only as long, and as far, as the benevolence does. Don't blink; you might miss it.

I Don't Know Why I Put Up with You: The Pennsylvania Story

The English Quaker leader William Penn, like George Calvert, parlayed a royal debt into a colony. Like Calvert, he assumed it would be a place where he and his fellow believers could always worship in peace. And, like Calvert, he was mistaken.

Penn got his charter for Pennsylvania in 1681 and set right to work devising a government for it. He drafted the original Frame of Government the next year, with a rambling preface that said, in essence, if Adam hadn't sinned we wouldn't need government at all, but since he had, we do. He added that he couldn't really settle on any one existing model of government and, anyway, each was only as good as the people that served in it, so what the heck. Not having grounded his government beyond these observations, he then plunged into governing and, in a series of "laws agreed on," granted certain liberties. Among them was the provision that anyone who believed in God and obeyed the law would "in no wayes be molested or prejudiced for their religious Perswasion or Practice."

For all its lack of precision (and its exclusion of nonbelievers), it was still a magnificent gesture. Penn had himself been imprisoned in the Tower of London for being a Quaker. And here he had his own colony and there was no lack of Quakers to populate it. (Four years later, eight thousand Quakers had already moved there.) Who could have blamed Penn if he'd established a narrow and stingy tolerance *à la* the separatists in Plymouth?

But Penn was no Pilgrim. He was determined to welcome a broad range of believers into his colony. In fact, he advertised for them in Europe with pamphlets written in French, German and Dutch. Many oppressed minorities responded, beginning with German and Swiss Mennonites and including the exotic-sounding Dunkards, Schwenkfelders and Moravians. Eccentrics were welcomed, too. One group even "lived in caves along the banks of the Wissahickon Creek, awaiting the 'Woman of the Wilderness,' whose arrival would usher in the millennium."

Nevertheless, tolerance proved as mutable in Pennsylvania as anywhere else. In 1705, the colonial assembly bowed to English pressure and barred Jews and Catholics from public office. This law would remain on the books until it was abolished (sort of, but we'll get to that) by Pennsylvania's new constitution in 1776.

The colonial assembly became the site of a power struggle among various religious groups; by 1756 the once-dominant Quakers had deserted the assembly altogether. And the assorted faiths weren't always sure what to do about each other: Lutherans and Anglicans intrigued against each other, as distrustful of the Quakers as the Quakers were of them. The influx of German settlers (the same settlers Penn had encouraged with his advertisements) became the source of great suspicion among the colonists. Not only were many of them pacifist, they were, well, German. So the colonists did what any sensible seventeenth-century Englishman would do—made them take an oath. Any German entering the colonies had to enter his name on a register and take an oath of allegiance to the king.

Oath or *affirmation*, right? No. The Quakers' withdrawal from public life had come with consequences: oath requirements and conscription. Quakers in Pennsylvania learned the hard way the same lesson their fellow idealists had learned, also the hard way: tolerance lacks staying power. At bottom, it's just a political act, so it can be undone politically at any moment.

Revolutionary Pennsylvania reinforced this point. Its proposed constitution once again, with its left hand, extended toleration to anyone who "acknowledges the being of a God." It then took it back again with its right: it set out test oaths excluding all but Christians from the legislature.

The instability of Pennsylvania's religious freedom can be traced in part to its original Frame of Government. William

Penn, though he was expansive in granting freedom of religion, never quite worked out just what he meant by the term (any more than he did by the term "government" itself). In practice, then, his freedom of religion became just another variation on the theme of tolerance: the government will put up with you for now, but things could always change.

In his own writings, Penn was more generous. He proposed extending toleration to Jews and Catholics—anyone who acknowledged the one God. But his reasoning was more parochial. Penn was, of course, a Quaker, who believed that each person was guided by the "Inner Light," the Spirit of God within oneself. Penn argued that to persecute someone in matters of conscience was to invade the prerogative of God, attempting to dim the Inner Light. Regulation of acts of worship, likewise, invaded God's territory by assuming governance over something that belonged only to Him. A great argument for convincing Quakers—who weren't the problem and didn't need convincing. A very poor argument for convincing everybody else.

Penn had more pragmatic reasoning as well. After a stint in the Tower of London, he wrote that it was the "worst argument in the world to convince me, for whoever was in the wrong those who used force for religion never could be in the right." Also a good point, except against people who make their converts the old-fashioned way: They coerce them.

In short, Penn's heart was very much in the right place. But in practice, his "I-know-it-when-I-see-it" theory of freedom still doesn't get us there. It offers a nice basis for those willing to accept his central assertions about God, and it provides us with the pragmatic observation that religious persecution breeds stalwarts, not converts. It is a basis to end persecution, but not to recognize inalienable rights—as the people of Pennsylvania learned the hard way.

I'm Putting Up with You Only Because God Told Me To: The Rhode Island Story

Rhode Island was perhaps the most imaginative experiment in

tolerance of its time. But ultimately, it still failed. Its problem, though, was different from Maryland's and Pennsylvania's. Each of those colonies announced a program of tolerance without ever bothering to tie it down publicly to anything other than the founder's authority and goodwill. So when the storm came, tolerance simply blew away. Rhode Island, by contrast, tied it down to more than just the founder's will. Unfortunately, what authorities there tied it down to was God's will, and successor governments didn't agree on what that was.

Providence Plantations, as Rhode Island was then known, was a scruffy little settlement that was continually scrambling to stay one step ahead of its various pursuers. It was founded in 1636 by Roger Williams, whom we met in Chapter Four as he was being kicked out of the Massachusetts Bay Colony. While the leaders of the Bay Colony and Plymouth Colony were considering what to do about the heretical and unruly "Islanders," Williams managed to secure an initial patent. Later, in 1663, he obtained a royal charter that said the new colony should be a "livlie experiment, that a most flourishing civill state may...best bee maintained...with a full livertie in religious concernements...." Significantly, the king's charter noted the limited potential for mischief in such liberty because of the great distance of the colony from England. He might have added that its founder, for all his genius, was a little flaky.

Flaky, but principled. As we saw in Chapter Four, Williams had gotten himself kicked out of Massachusetts Bay in large part because he had refused to be in communion with those he considered impure. His views didn't change in his new settlement. In Providence, Williams founded the first Baptist church in America, served as its first minister—and promptly separated from it three months later because his own church wasn't pure enough for him. Eventually he separated from everyone except his wife and worshipped alone with her in their house. Nevertheless, as fastidious as he was, Williams was willing to welcome into his colony all sorts of people with whom he would never dream of being in communion, including Jews.

Why was Williams so tolerant? Because he believed it was God's will that Christians not persecute others. "Forced worship," he said, "stinks in God's nostrils." On the contrary, "it is the will and command of God" for "permission of the most paganish, Jewish, Turkish, or antichristian consciences and worships, [to] be granted to all men in all nations and countries." In other words, where the Pilgrims and Puritans believed that theological truth required them to restrict others' freedom, Williams believed just the opposite. For him, theological truth required that he guarantee freedom even to those who were mistaken.

This was, of course, a great step forward. A Christianity committed to tolerance was better and more Christian than one bent on persecution. In fact, Williams got much about religious liberty right. Most importantly, he saw that it was morally wrong to coerce people's consciences in religious matters. Nevertheless, there was at least one serious problem with Williams' theory: *Why* such broad religious freedom? What was the central argument that could be deployed effectively against Winthrop in the Bay Colony, the Anglicans in England, or any other skeptics in need of convincing?

Williams' answer was that it was "the command of God" that consciences not be coerced. Once again, that's a magnificent insight, but a miserable argument. It convinces only those who share the insight itself. It's positively hopeless against the likes of Winthrop, people who have no doubt that God's will is something completely different. In fact, it seems almost self-defeating: it likely will fail to convince the very "paganish" and "antichristian consciences" it is destined to attract. In fact, it did have a short shelf life: successor governments of Rhode Island, which did not share in Williams' revelation, felt free to cut back on the religious liberty he recognized.

I'll Put Up with Yours If You Put Up with Mine: John Locke in Theory and Practice

Carolina (not yet a North and a South) was on a different page altogether. Where Maryland didn't know it needed a theory of tolerance, Pennsylvania couldn't settle on one and Rhode Island based its on theology, Carolina was founded as an early experiment in social contract theory. In an odd (and often overlooked) twist of history, John Locke, the preeminent philosopher of the English Enlightenment, drafted most of the Constitution of Carolina, in 1669.

Locke's constitution stressed the need to tolerate other faiths—all other faiths—in order that "civil peace may be maintained amidst diversity of opinions, and our agreement and compact with all men may be duly and faithfully observed." Accordingly, any seven people who acknowledged that there is a God, said that He should be worshipped publicly, and came up with a way to swear or affirm or do just about anything to attest to the truthfulness of their testimony could join together and form a religious assembly, provided that they registered it with the government.

To the colonial authorities, or "proprietors," this utopian vision was all well and good—provided that one didn't take it too seriously. Thus, over Locke's objections, the constitution also stipulated that the Church of England would be the established church of the land and could receive public funds.

And they were serious about this. By 1704, newly separate South Carolina passed a law ensuring an all-Anglican assembly. Not only that, but only Anglican ministers could perform marriages. (This requirement was not in effect in North Carolina, so dissenters simply sneaked their children across the border to be married in their own church—much to the consternation of local magistrates.) Licensing requirements were another issue, as new groups of separate Baptists arose, many unwilling to apply for licenses. The government didn't know what to do about this. After all, they'd agreed to tolerate the churches, even offered them government licenses. What could they do with someone who demanded freedom, not license?

The problem was particularly severe for Catholics, whom Carolinians feared "almost to a mania." The colony barred them from bearing arms until 1775. They were also barred from incorporating churches and voting.

The South Carolina constitution of 1776 represented both a victory and a defeat. The much-opposed establishment of the Anglican church was finally ended, and in its place an establishment of "all denominations of Christian protestants."

Catholics and Jews were tolerated, but not allowed to legally incorporate. In fact, no legal Mass was said in Charleston until 1790. North Carolina did no better: Jews would not be permitted to hold office there until 1868.

So what happened to the social contract that Locke had envisioned? To understand what went wrong in Carolina, we have to understand what was continuing to go wrong in England. England was embroiled in religious turmoil that would mark the whole of the seventeenth century. This all culminated in the "Glorious Revolution" as William and Mary took the throne and ushered in the so-called Act of Toleration in 1689. This act affirmed the establishment of the Church of England and provided broad freedoms for *Protestant* dissenters. Catholics still need not apply.

The ideology behind this limitation can be found in Locke. He wrote in his famous *Letter Concerning Toleration* that "neither pagan nor Mohametan nor Jew ought to be excluded from the civil rights of the commonwealth, because of his religion." But he footnoted his *Letter* with two notable exceptions: atheists and Catholics.

Locke's idea of toleration was informed by his conception of the social contract. Atheists, he thought, couldn't be trusted to keep contracts or swear oaths because they didn't have the prospect of eternal damnation to keep them honest. Catholics, he said, owed their true allegiance to the pope, a "foreign prince," and therefore couldn't be trusted to support the government of any non-Catholic nation. And if you couldn't trust someone to tolerate you, then you shouldn't tolerate them.

So religious liberty still wasn't a right that people possessed merely because of who they were. Even in enlightened theory it was something that the government could and sometimes should withhold from entire categories of people. And once the government withheld some, it was all too easy to withhold more and more.

Who Can Stand It?

As the colonial period drew to a close, we were poised on the eve of a revolution that would change all that had come before. The not-quite-nascent nation was a patchwork of colonies with wildly divergent ideas about the nature of freedom. They were eager for it, certainly, but what did freedom mean? And who was entitled to it? In Plymouth, freedom was a gift of God, but one given only to the true believers. So only the "freemen," those who were members of the official church, had any. This meant, at one point, that only 230 out of its 3,000 residents could even vote. The refuge colonies, for a variety of different reasons, extended tolerance more broadly—until they changed their minds. In sum, the colonial notions of religious freedom ranged between the appalling and the inadequate. Intolerance had proved to be too cruel, and tolerance too temporary. We needed a better idea.

Part Two

Groping for a Right

From Tolerance to Natural Rights

Reflections on the battle for
disestablishment in Virginia

J ames Madison had had enough of tolerance. It was now
eighty-five years since the English Parliament had passed the
Act of Toleration, lessening the persecution that dissenting
Protestants had weathered. And here there were six Baptist
preachers in jail in Culpepper County, Virginia, for preaching
without a license. The British regime had ordered the colonists
to allow such dissent, so long as the dissenting ministers registered with the government. But this was something that separate
Baptists could not in conscience do. Their right to preach, they
insisted, came from God and they neither needed nor would
seek the approval of any mere civil authorities. So some two
generations after the beginnings of official toleration, the six
were languishing in jail because they were still beyond its pale.
And beyond the pale of official toleration lay the same old
official persecution—which continued to do its work with a
vengeance. In another famous case, an unlicensed Baptist minister had been caught leading a prayer meeting in a field in
Caroline County, Virginia. As he was singing a hymn, the sheriff and an Anglican cleric rode up, gagged him with a bullwhip
and dragged him off to be flogged.

Madison was fed up. Writing to a college friend, he boiled
over at the

> diabolical Hell conceived principle of persecution.... This vexes
> me the most of any thing whatever. There are at this [time] in the
> adjacent County not less than 5 or 6 well meaning men in close

Gaol for publishing their religious Sentiments which in the main are very orthodox. I have neither the patience to hear talk or think of anything relative to this matter for I have squabbled and scolded, abused and ridiculed so long about it, to so little purpose that I am without common patience. So...pity me and pray for Liberty of Conscience.

Soon, though, Madison got the chance to do more than just squabble and scold. It was the spring of 1776, and the twenty-five-year-old Madison had just been appointed to the Virginia legislature's committee in charge of preparing a declaration of rights for the commonwealth. He seized the opportunity to do something bold: He framed religious freedom, not as the fruit of tolerance, but as a right. George Mason, the chairman of the committee, had submitted a draft that included the assertion that "all Men shou'd enjoy the fullest *Toleration* in the Exercise of Religion, according to the Dictates of Conscience...." The chairman no doubt thought he was being broad-minded in according toleration to all and not just to some. Madison, however, wouldn't stand for it. Not only had he witnessed toleration's failure in practice, he had a better idea in principle. He secured an amendment to the draft, deleting toleration and replacing it with the phrase "all men are *equally entitled to the full and free exercise* of [religion], according to the dictates of Conscience." He thus framed the "free exercise" of religion as an entitlement of all, not a result of the government's benevolence.

And, as if that weren't provocative enough, he went further, insisting that the right to free exercise of religion necessarily implied disestablishing the official church. So he added language to do just that. "No man or class of men," his draft had it, "ought, on account of religion to be invested with peculiar emoluments or privileges."

The full text, as Madison had redrafted it, said it was a "truth":

> That Religion, or the Duty which we owe to our Creator, and the Manner of discharging it, can be governed only by Reason and Conviction, not by Compulsion or Violence; and therefore all men are equally entitled to the full and free exercise of it according to the dictates of Conscience, unpunished and unrestrained

by the Magistrate, unless under Colour of Religion any Man disturb the Peace, the Happiness, or Safety of Society, or of Individuals; and therefore that no man or class of man ought, on account of religion to be invested with peculiar emoluments or privileges. And that it is the mutual Duty of all, to practice Christian Forbearance, Love and Charity towards Each other.

Madison's draft was a legal and philosophical lightning strike. The firestorm it touched off in Virginia raged for nearly a decade as Madison's fellow legislators welcomed the rhetoric of rights but preferred the flexibility of tolerance. Why couldn't they have it both ways? Where did this "free exercise" stuff come from anyway? And was it really necessary to take it so very seriously?

The story of Madison's pivot from tolerance to free exercise, and of the reaction it provoked, helps us reflect on these questions—and on the adequacy of the Pilgrims' and the Park Rangers' notions of religious freedom.

It's a Truth, Sort of...

Madison's fellow legislators were of two minds about his draft. They were happy to proclaim it a "truth" that "religion...can be governed only by reason and conviction." They just didn't want to live with the consequences of this truth. So Patrick Henry, who had introduced the amendment on Madison's behalf but was not the brightest light on the colonial tree, was formally asked if the amendment was intended to disestablish the church. This should have been a who's-buried-in-Grant's-tomb kind of question. Of course it was intended to disestablish the church. Henry, though, was taken aback and said "No." The amendment was then sent back for redrafting to make sure it left the established church in its privileged position.

Chagrined, Madison compromised as little as possible, deleting only the line banning the government from granting "emoluments or privileges" on account of religion. The redraft passed. The anomalous result therefore was that the Virginia legislature solemnly proclaimed it to be the "truth" that the manner of discharging one's obligation to God was solely a matter of conscience, while leaving at least formally intact the establishment of the Anglican church along with many of its supporting laws.

Those laws entitled the church to substantial government assistance. Taxpayers paid the salaries of Anglican clergy in Virginia. And those who failed to uphold crucial Christian tenets suffered, at least in theory, substantial legal disabilities. According to colonial statutes in Virginia, neither atheists nor those who denied the doctrine of the Trinity nor those who questioned the authority of Scripture could hold public office, receive a gift or legacy, execute a will, or act as executor of an estate. They could not even be the legal guardians of their own children. Furthermore, English common law retained its force in Virginia, so in theory anyway, judges could still sentence heretics to burn at the stake. The legislature was willing to speak the language of rights, so long as it hung on to the perquisites of tolerance.

The legislature's inconsistency sets in high relief the differences between tolerance and a natural right to religious liberty. Notice the idea underlying Madison's draft: The shape of freedom follows from the shape of human nature, not from the extent of the government's largesse. From what we know of who we are—in this case, that "the Duty which we owe to our Creator" can properly be discharged only in freedom—we can derive moral constraints on the use of coercion—here, that all are "equally entitled" to the free exercise of religion "according to the dictates of conscience." In other words, because our minds and consciences function well only when they are uncoerced, it is wrong to coerce them.

That was a very different idea from the tolerance that the lawmakers were used to. It wasn't selective; it didn't apply only to some favored types of heretics, as in Maryland. It wasn't conditioned on any sort of government approval or license, as it had been in Virginia up till then. It wasn't limited, as Locke would have had it, to those you could count on to tolerate you in return should they ever come to power. It wasn't revocable, as it had been in all those venues. It was none of these things because it was based on a different premise from all of them. For Madison, religious liberty could be neither revoked nor restricted, "unless under Colour of Religion any Man disturb the Peace, the Happiness, or Safety of Society, or of Individuals." It was based on something that could itself be neither revoked nor restricted: human reason and conscience.

Madison's conclusions were thus similar to those of Roger Williams, though they were based on a different premise. Williams' argument was a theological one: everyone had religious freedom because God had revealed it to be so. His argument therefore was convincing only to those who shared its premise of God's revelation. Madison's argument, by contrast, was based not on theology but on human nature, albeit a human nature that was presumed to seek God—indeed, to be duty-bound to do so. It thus had a far broader potential reach. (Nevertheless, its reach was still restricted by its unargued assumption, that all experience a hunger and have a duty to seek God. This premise could be taken for granted in the eighteenth century. For better or worse, it can't be today. We'll try to remedy this weakness later in the book.)

Notice also what the idea of rights, as opposed to tolerance, means for legislators: There are certain things they may not do, ever. Most matters of government are subject to the rough-and-tumble of ordinary politics. How much we are taxed, how public funds should be spent, what regulations to impose on businesses are all questions on which reasonable people may differ. There is usually no better way for the various competing interests in any society to hash out their differences and reach some kind of peaceful compromise than for elected representatives to work things out in a legislative assembly. Human rights, though, claim immunity from this kind of compromise. On the contrary, they claim to impose moral limits on what the government may otherwise ordinarily do. It doesn't matter how strong or how clever a legislative consensus emerges—if it does not respect the equal right to religious liberty, it is illegitimate.

Legislators, though, tend to bristle at the idea that there are things they may not do. And "illegitimate" is such a harsh word. Whether it's because of some principle that they believe is more important, or out of an overriding sense of pragmatism, or purely due to pride, legislators often experience a certain claustrophobia when they're around human rights arguments.

Thus, the Virginia legislators were happy to proclaim "the truth" about free exercise. And they seem to have meant it; there is no reason to suppose they were lying. Nevertheless, they simply refused to be bound by the implications of the truth they had proclaimed. They thought they should be free to say, at one and the same time, that there was a natural right to freedom of religion—and that it could properly be compromised in the usual sort of legislative horse-trading. Natural rights were fine as long as you didn't take them too seriously.

(This is a lesson that Madison would remember—though not well enough—when it came time to draft a federal bill of rights. We'll face that disappointment in Chapter Nine.)

Enter Thomas Jefferson

Meanwhile, the battle in Virginia was far from over. Thomas Jefferson, who from 1776 to 1779 served as a representative in the Virginia House of Delegates, was appalled by the inconsistent network of laws that survived the Declaration of Rights. He proposed to clean up the mess in dramatic fashion with his own "Bill for Establishing Religious Freedom."

Jefferson's bill began with a celebrated preamble that echoed Madison's thinking on religious liberty. "Almighty God," it famously declared, "hath created the mind free." It could not be affected either "by temporal punishments, burdens or incapacities," or "by worldly honors or emoluments." Compelling support of religion was "sinful and tyrannical" and "a departure from the plan of the Holy author of our religion, who being Lord both of body and mind, yet chose not to propagate it by coercions on either." Moreover, left to its own devices, the truth would out.

The bill also contained an equally celebrated postscript that declared religious liberty to be a natural right:

> And though we well know that this Assembly, elected by the people for the ordinary purposes of legislation only, have no

power to restrain the acts of succeeding Assemblies, constituted with powers equal to our own, and that therefore to declare this act irrevocable, would be of no effect in law; yet we are free to declare, and do declare, that the rights hereby asserted are of the natural rights of mankind, and that if any act shall be hereafter passed to repeal the present or to narrow its operation, such act will be an infringement of natural right.

In between, Jefferson's bill sought to remove the state from the regulation of religion entirely by ensuring that no one was either punished or rewarded for his or her religious beliefs and that no one was compelled to attend or support any worship or ministry.

The legislature, however, did not go along with Jefferson any more than it had with Madison. They buried the bill in one committee, discharged that committee, then instructed a different committee (but one that included Madison) to rethink the whole subject. Then, when Madison's committee recommended a bill that almost completely disestablished the Anglican church, the legislature reduced the key clause—the one abolishing state pay for the clergy—to a mere suspension. This latest compromise again left standing what was becoming an increasingly rickety establishment.

It also left Patrick Henry more convinced than ever that this free exercise stuff was getting out of hand.

The Establishment Strikes Back

He bided his time. Then, some five years later (and with Jefferson safely out of the way as ambassador to Paris), Patrick Henry counterattacked by introducing a bill to levy a state property tax, the proceeds of which would go to *all* "teachers of the Gospel." Henry may not have been brilliant but he was certainly shrewd. Rather than try to re-fund the Anglican church (now known in America as the "Protestant Episcopal Church"), Henry proposed to use government money to support *all* Protestant churches. Thus all faiths stood to benefit (Jews, Catholics and nonbelievers remaining, as was usual, politically insignificant minorities). Furthermore, under Henry's bill, each individual taxpayer would himself be able to choose to which church he wanted to send his share of the tax. Nobody, therefore (except the politically insignificant), could complain that the tax violated his or her freedom of conscience. Henry thereby put himself on the side of all Protestants in Virginia. At the same time, he also forced Madison to explain why *free exercise of religion* necessitated *disestablishment* of it. Even Madison's absent ally Thomas Jefferson, who was following events from Paris, had to admire what he called "the exquisite cunning of the old fox."

Ideas Really Do Have Consequences

The controversy over Henry's bill proved to be a great opportunity. And Madison took full advantage of it. Having managed to table the bill until the following year, he wrote and circulated a petition opposing it, called a "Memorial and Remonstrance Against Religious Assessments." The "Memorial and Remonstrance" is the most systematic account of Madison's thought on religious liberty. It lays out his theory of the relationship between natural rights and legal ones. And it responds to Patrick Henry's challenge: Why does the natural right to free exercise of religion forbid establishment of it?

As to the first point, Madison believed that natural rights weren't limited by legal ones. If there's one thing that the legislative history of the Declaration of Rights shows, it's that it wasn't intended to block public support of even one privileged church, much less of all Protestant churches generally. The law was against him. Nevertheless, Madison did not hesitate to argue that Henry's bill violated the natural right of religious liberty itself. Thus, it was not only the law, it was "a fundamental and undeniable truth, 'that religion or the duty which we owe to our Creator and the manner of discharging it, can be directed only by reason and conviction.'" And so: "The Religion then of every man must be left to the conviction and conscience of every man; and it is the *right* of every man to *exercise* it as these may dictate." For Madison, the "exercise" of religion was what one had a natural right to. Or, in other words, "free exercise" was Madison's shorthand for the natural right to religious freedom. And it wasn't restricted to what the legislature had chosen to codify.

What did Madison imagine the "free exercise" of this right would look like? Much more than the Pilgrims' grudging allowance for dissidents to believe in private. And more than toleration, which allowed certain dissidents a limited license to believe in public. No, Madison would not settle for anything less than for everyone to have the "freedom to *embrace,* to *profess* and to *observe* the Religion which we believe to be of divine origin.*" That is, everyone would have the right to believe ("to embrace") what seemed to him or her to be true, to express ("to profess") those beliefs and try to convince others of them, and then to live according to ("to observe") those beliefs.

And it would be a universal right, possessed even by those we are convinced are wrong. Because we claim this right for ourselves, Madison argued, "we cannot deny an equal freedom to those whose minds have not yet yielded to the evidence which has convinced us." They have the right to be wrong.

Moreover, this "right is in its nature an unalienable right," that is, a right we may not even voluntarily surrender. Why? In large part, Madison says,

> because what is here a right towards men, is a duty towards the Creator. It is the duty of every man to render to the Creator such homage and such only as he believes to be acceptable to him. This duty is precedent, both in order of time and in degree of obligation, to the claims of Civil Society. Before any man can be considered as a member of Civil Society, he must be considered as a subject of the Governour of the Universe: And if a member of Civil Society, do it with a saving of his allegiance to the Universal Sovereign.

In short, Madison says that because we each have a duty to follow our minds and consciences toward the Creator, and because this duty comes before our obligations to the state, it cannot be interfered with by the State except in extreme circumstances. "We maintain therefore that in matters of Religion," concluded Madison, "no man's right is abridged by the institution of Civil Society and that Religion is wholly exempt from its cognizance." And so, for free exercise's sake, establishments are out of the question.

The "Memorial and Remonstrance" gained the support of 1,522 signatories, which, combined with other petitions, totaled 10,929 petitioners against Henry's bill. In November 1785, Henry's plan was "crushed." In the aftermath of this success, Madison was able to carry Jefferson's long-stalled bill through the Virginia legislature in almost exactly the same form in which it had been mothballed in 1779. As we have seen, it too proclaimed religious liberty a natural right that had its own force even apart from legislation.

Madison's Legacy

Madison insisted that from fundamental facts of human nature we derive rights that no government, even one acting through elected representatives, may justly transgress. Largely as a result, it is now a settled part of our national ethos that religious liberty is such a right.

It is so settled, in fact, that our Pilgrims and Park Rangers all feel obligated to pay it lip service, much as Madison's contemporaries did. Ask either faction whether it believes religious liberty is a human right and you'll get a passionate, tub-thumping—mostly hypocritical—speech in favor of the idea. That's because religious freedom is so familiar, so American a concept that nobody can really admit to opposing it. That would be like opposing apple pie. So even those who are at each other's throats over religious liberty have to insist they all absolutely love the stuff. Instead of confessing that they're actually opposed to religious freedom for all, the Pilgrims and the Park Rangers among us equivocate. When they say they support "religious freedom," the Pilgrims mean the freedom of *their* religion, while the Park Rangers mean freedom *from others'* religions. That way, they can all sound so very American—they can say they're in favor of something called religious freedom—and still be as oppressive as they want to be.

Both sorts of extremists take refuge in the resulting confusion. Insisting on answers to the fundamental questions—what is religious liberty, where does it come from and what difference does that make—smokes them out. It exposes their hypocrisy on the subject of human rights just as it exposed the confusion of the Virginia legislators.

These are the questions on which we'll focus in the rest of the book. We'll begin with a story of a most unlikely villain: religious liberty's erstwhile hero, Thomas Jefferson.

EIGHT

Inalienable Rights, Slightly Alienated

Reflections on Thomas Jefferson
in public and in private

The Author was editing. It was the summer of 1776 and Thomas Jefferson was revising his draft Declaration of Independence. With a little help from his friends Benjamin Franklin and John Adams, he changed "sacred and undeniable" to "self-evident," and "rights inherent" to "inalienable rights." So now the Declaration said that it was a "self-evident" truth that "all men are created equal" and are "endowed by their Creator with certain inalienable rights." There. That would damn the British.

And Jefferson, too. On the day Jefferson wrote that it was "self-evident" that all are "created equal," he owned over 175 slaves. On the day he died half a century later, he owned even more—about 200. In between, he had freed only 3, while selling at least 85. Even in his will, he freed only 5 more of his slaves, leaving the remaining 200 or so in bondage, many of them sold to pay his debts. During his lifetime, the author of the Declaration of Independence owned at least 315 different human beings—all of whom he had *said* were created equal to him.

Whether he really *believed* they were equal to him is a different matter. His other writings, and his behavior, suggest not. And slavery wasn't the only fissure between Jefferson's natural rights rhetoric and his life. As we'll see, there was a large gap on the subject of religion as well. It's not a pretty story. Was Jefferson a hypocrite? Was he philosophically confused? Both? And, more importantly, what difference does it make? Is a public argument undermined by the failings of its author, or does it have a force all its own?

Pondering the distance between the public and the private Jefferson helps answer at least that last question (and sheds light on the others). And that last question is an especially important one since both Pilgrims and Park Rangers claim Jefferson as their patron saint, quoting him selectively and largely ignoring the contradictions.

Jefferson's story also points up a limitation in rights arguments themselves. Bald appeals to human rights that are said to follow self-evidently from human nature are not enough. To argue for a human right, one must be specific. One must identify what it is about our common humanity that establishes moral boundaries that others may not transgress, and then link the contours of these boundaries to the contours of our humanity. Otherwise we risk being unpersuasive at best and an absolute menace at worst. Skipping this step is dangerous. Without it, even the Jeffersons of this world can badly stray.

Do as I Say...

It wasn't just the Declaration of Independence. And it wasn't just the sort of slaveholding that was common in Jefferson's Virginia. The gap between Jefferson's public argument and his private behavior on slavery runs much deeper. In his magnum opus, *Notes on the State of Virginia,* Jefferson publicly condemned the importation of slaves. "In the very first session held under the republican government," he boasted, "the assembly passed a law for the perpetual prohibition of the importation of slaves." Jefferson said he hoped that a ban on importing slaves would "stop the increase of this great political and moral evil, while the minds of our citizens may be ripening for a complete emancipation of human nature." The trouble is, on the day Jefferson first published these words, which he had printed at his own expense while he was in Paris, he was enjoying the services of James Hemings, a slave whom he himself had imported into France, where slavery was illegal. Then he did it again. Jefferson arranged for his slave (and his late wife's half-sister) Sally Hemings to be brought over to serve him as well. Much has been made about the affair that Jefferson likely had with her. Far too little is made of the fact that he kept his half-sister-in-law illegally enslaved in France in the first place.

Jefferson knew exactly what he was doing, too. On August 25, 1786, he wrote to reassure Paul Bentalou, an American who had also brought a slave with him to France and was now concerned that the slave might go free. Jefferson told him to relax. He knew, he said, obviously referring to himself, about another "instance where a person bringing in a slave, and saying nothing about it, has not been disturbed in his possession." What's more, said Jefferson, the slave will likely be ignorant of the law and not know enough to demand his or her freedom. In other words, there was no need to worry about any inalienable rights inconveniently asserting themselves.

What on earth, you may ask, had gotten into the author of the Declaration of Independence?

Devout Jeffersonians, faced with having to defend the indefensible, argue that Jefferson was merely bending to the hypocrisy of his times. But this everyone-else-was-doing-it defense seems particularly unworthy of a man famous for being *sui generis*. If ever there was a man immune from peer pressure, it would be Thomas Jefferson. Hypocrisy certainly seems to be part of it, but there must be more to the story as well.

There is another, darker explanation for Jefferson's inconsistency. It wasn't just personal weakness. It was a profound moral and philosophical error—one that we should learn from, so as not to repeat. We assume that Jefferson would have subscribed to the following syllogism: all men are created equal, slaves and slave-masters are both men, slaves and their masters are therefore equal to one another. Masters should thus free their slaves. The trouble is, Jefferson skipped the second step. He never said slaves were as fully "men" as their masters were, and, strange as it sounds, he doesn't seem to have believed it.

African slaves, he thought, were greater than beasts but inferior to whites, and as such, not capable of the same liberty. Jefferson saw clearly that slaves were at least destined for freedom: "Nothing is more certainly written in the book of fate," he wrote in his autobiography, "than that these people are to be free." But he did not believe that the two races could ever live together on equal terms, for, in his words, "nature, habit, opinion has drawn indelible lines of distinction between them."

Jefferson's views on those "indelible lines" are infamous. Africans, he thought, were fundamentally different from whites. They "participate more of sensation than reflection." African slaves, Jefferson said, were not distinguished in art, science or literature as compared with Roman slaves; they did not have advanced thinking skills; unlike the Native Americans, they had neither poetry nor art nor imagination. What's more, they had "a very strong and disagreeable odor," though they did "require less sleep" than whites. And they were brave—but only because they lacked forethought, so they could not anticipate danger.

How much of this did Jefferson think was real racial inferiority as opposed to lack of opportunity? A great deal, or so say his thoughts on sexuality. Sexually, he said, African men preferred white women "as uniformly as is the preference of the Oran-utan for the black woman over those of his species." Jefferson plainly thought "nature" rather than "habit and opinion" had drawn most of the "indelible lines" separating the races.

Jefferson's pronouncement that "all men are created equal" launched a revolution that continues to this day, but his own views as to who was included in "all men" handicapped his imagination. It is an important lesson: arguments from human nature can't be vaguely general or else they leave room for even the geniuses of the world to misunderstand them—to mistake the scope of those rights by mistaking the scope of human nature itself. When that happens, the result is a right that just doesn't function properly. It's either a right that doesn't cover everything, or, as in Jefferson's case, a right that doesn't cover every*one*. As Jefferson himself illustrated, the consequences may be tragic.

There are, then, two lessons to be drawn from Jefferson and slavery. The first is not to skip steps in an argument on human rights. The second is that public arguments have their own force and should be taken on their own terms, regardless of the limitations—or even downright hypocrisy—of their authors. Jefferson's behavior was reprehensible, yet this callousness toward the rights of his slaves does not diminish the force of the public argument he made. He was right—all are created equal—even if he didn't quite believe it himself.

I Do Believe I Don't

The gap between the public and the private Jefferson extended beyond the subject of slavery. There was likewise a disconnect on the subject of religion. Jefferson's public arguments were out of sync with his private views, and his behavior was inconsistent with both. But just as Jefferson's philosophical limitations and sheer weakness do not somehow qualify the idea that "all men are created equal," neither do Jefferson's inconsistencies on religion diminish the force of his public arguments for religious liberty.

Jefferson's Public Argument on Religious Liberty

Jefferson's most extended public argument for religious liberty was in his Virginia Bill for Establishing Religious Freedom, which we encountered in the last chapter. He drafted it in 1779; it passed, in his absence, in 1786.

In his bill, Jefferson makes three related but distinct arguments, the first of which is the most interesting and far-reaching. The argument: "Almighty God hath created the mind free …[and] all attempts to influence it by temporal punishments or burthens, or by civil incapacitations, tend only to beget habits of hypocrisy and meanness…." It's a subtle point, but an important (and very Madisonian) one. He's saying that religious liberty arises from the shape of human nature—from the fact that we each have a free mind that rebels against being coerced and demands instead to be persuaded. Our free minds and our unwillingness to bend—that pesky call of conscience—tell us something vital about ourselves: that we were made for freedom. Liberty follows logically from who we are. A people with free minds, who find themselves duty-bound to follow their consciences no matter what the cost, ought to be free to do so. It's the lesson of Mary Dyer and Roger Williams—that conscience, however strange its calls may be, is to be respected. The consequence of a naturally free mind is a natural right to freedom.

Jefferson's next two points are less momentous. In fact, each tells us more about Jefferson than it does about religious liberty. His second point is a crowd-pleaser. Attempts at coercion, he writes, "are a departure from the plan of the Holy author of our religion, who being Lord both of body and mind, yet chose not to propagate it by coercions on either." By choosing free will over forced worship, the Holy author set the example. What the Lord himself had refused to do, government had no right to attempt.

Let's pause for a moment to consider an interesting question. Who was the "Holy author," and what was "our religion"? The Virginia legislature of the time would naturally take this as a reference to Jesus and Christianity. But when an amendment to make this explicit failed, Jefferson was gleeful. As he recounts in his autobiography, "Where the preamble declares, that coercion is a departure from the plan of the holy author of our religion, an amendment was proposed by inserting 'Jesus Christ,' so that it would read 'A departure from the plan of Jesus Christ, the holy author of our religion;' the insertion was rejected by the great majority, in proof that they meant to comprehend, within the mantel of its protection, the Jew and the Gentile, the Christian and Mohametan, the Hindoo, and infidel of every denomination."

So, who was the *holy author,* and what was *our religion?* Jefferson never says, and with good reason. As we will see in a moment, Jefferson's private correspondence makes clear that there was not any holy author of any religion he could accurately describe as "ours." Nevertheless, invoking such a concept was a telling argument in the minds of his fellow legislators, and that seems to have been enough for him.

The third argument is vintage Jefferson: "...that truth is great and will prevail if left to herself, that she is the proper and sufficient antagonist to error and has nothing to fear from the conflict, unless by human interposition disarmed of her natural weapons, free argument and debate, errors ceasing to be dangerous when it is permitted freely to contradict them." Taken together, and at face value, the second and third arguments reinforce one another. God doesn't coerce, so neither should we. Instead, we should let truth and error battle, and truth will win. It reads like William Penn with a splash of John Milton.

In short, the public Jefferson argued that religious liberty was an inalienable right because it was inherent in a universal human nature created so by God: it followed the example of the "Holy author of our religion," and it provided the best environment in which truth could flourish. By these lights, the public Jefferson seems almost conventional. He appears to be a supporter of religion generally and of Christianity in particular.

Hardly.

Jefferson's Private Views on Religion

For Jefferson, organized religion was the enemy. He quickly dismissed orthodox Christianity. The idea that Jesus was the Son of God made man was, to him, preposterous. As he wrote to John Adams, he thought the day would come "when the mystical generation of Jesus, by the Supreme Being as his father, in the womb of a virgin will be classed with the fable of the generation of Minerva in the brain of Jupiter." The Trinity was equally absurd, he said. Writing to James Smith, he dismissed "the hocus-pocus phantasm of a God...with one body and three heads." And to Adams he wrote: "It is too late in the day for men of sincerity to pretend they believe in the Platonic mysticism that three are one and one is three, and yet, that the one is not three, and the three are not one.... But this constitutes the craft, the power, and profit of the priests. Sweep away their gossamer fabrics of a fictitious religion, and they would catch no more flies."

Jefferson was every bit as dismissive of Judaism. The rabbis, he said, were "a bloodthirsty race, as cruel and remorseless as the being whom they represented as the family God of Abraham, of Isaac, and Jacob, and the local God of Israel." That God, he said, was "cruel, vindictive, capricious, and unjust."

Jefferson wrote similarly to John Adams, saying that the Jewish God "would be deemed a very indifferent man with us."

And it wasn't just the theology of those religions that Jefferson disagreed with. It was the whole idea of organized religion itself. Jefferson's private correspondence teems with denunciations of "priests," a term he used to encompass all leaders of organized religion, even those who would never refer to themselves that way. Such leaders, explained Jefferson privately to his friends, "perverted" Christianity "into an engine for enslaving mankind, a mere contrivance to filch wealth and power to themselves." Jefferson exhibited little of his famed optimism in the power of reason when it came to organized religion, for in his view priests can weave "spells" over their flocks, "moulding their minds as wax in the hollow of their hands." Priests encourage ignorance, for they "dread the advance of science as witches do the approach of daylight." And their self-interest is invariably against liberty: "In every country and in every age, the priest has been hostile to liberty. He is always in alliance with the despot, abetting his abuses in return for protection to his own." For Jefferson, organized religions and their "priests" were great obstacles to human flourishing that ought to be removed.

Thomas Jefferson, Demagogue

In the meantime, though, Jefferson also wanted to get elected. So in much the same way that Bill Clinton campaigned for governor of Arkansas by singing in the choir at televised church services, Jefferson said he was, too, religious. He insisted loudly that he was a "Christian," adding *sotto voce* that he was one "in the only sense in which [Jesus] wished anyone to be; sincerely attached to his doctrines, in preference to all others; ascribing to himself every *human* excellence; and believing he never claimed any other." In private: "It is not to be understood that I am with [Jesus] in all his doctrines. I am a Materialist."

Jefferson had good reason for this balancing act. In attempting to defeat his bid for the presidency in 1800, the Federalist Party tried to rouse popular indignation by accusing Jefferson of atheism and by insinuating that he was colluding with the French revolutionaries to eradicate Christianity. Why, asked Timothy Dwight of Yale College, should any Christian support "the philosophers, the atheists, and the deists" as represented by Jefferson? "Is it that our churches may become temples of reason, our Sabbath a decade, and our Psalms of praise Marseilles hymns? Is it that we may behold such a strumpet personating a goddess on the alter of Jehovah? Is it that we may see the Bible cast into a bonfire? ...Shall our sons become the disciples of Voltaire and the dragoons of Marat?" (And you thought today's attack ads were bad.) The *Gazette of the United States* was equally strident: "At the present solemn moment the only question to be asked by every American laying his hand on his heart, is Shall I continue in allegiance to God—and a religious president; or impiously declare for Jefferson—and no God!!!"

Now, through all the hyperbole, his critics were basically on to Thomas Jefferson. While he probably wasn't really an atheist, he was at most a deist. (Throughout his life he seems to have wandered back and forth across the line between deism and agnosticism.) And he really did despise organized religion.

Jefferson, though, remained formally an Episcopalian, attended church services, and contributed money to various churches. Nor did he shy away from public displays of religion, even when those displays took place under government roofs. Two days after he wrote his famed letter to the Danbury Baptist Association, in which he praised the "wall of separation" between church and state, Jefferson attended Sunday worship services held at the Capitol, on the floor of the House of Representatives, and brought along the Marine Band to accompany the hymns. In other words, Jefferson stood in the halls of Congress—a place he couldn't possibly have thought religious services belonged—in worship of someone he most emphatically did not believe was God. He even provided the music.

Jefferson's private antireligious sentiment did find one home in his public persona. He was not above playing to the anti-Catholic prejudices of his time. Connecticut's Congregationalism he called "a protestant popedom" that served only "to disgrace American history and character." And Virginia

Presbyterians "pant to re-establish by law, that holy inquisition which they can now only infuse into public opinion." Adopting the rhetoric of anti-Catholicism suited Jefferson's purpose. He deflected Protestant criticism of himself in part by using rhetorical code words suggesting that he and his listeners close ranks against the threat of creeping Catholicism.

Jefferson's claim to be a Christian, his attendance at services, and his appeals to popular sentiments satisfied the public just enough to parry the Federalist attack. They have done far less for his credibility.

Hypocrisy in Politics? ...Shocking

Well, so what? So what if Jefferson said one thing, but believed another? He was, after all, running for office, and we've long become accustomed to such dissonance on the part of candidates. But thinking through the disconnect between the public and the private Jefferson is important. One of the more amusing spectacles of the culture wars is the tug-of-war over Thomas Jefferson. Pilgrims have him by one arm, Park Rangers by the other, and both factions are trying to drag him into their camp.

Thus, there are Pilgrims who, amazingly, take his "I am a Christian" propaganda at face value, conveniently ignore the rest of his writings, and want everybody else to do the same. Their arguments can't be taken seriously.

Then there are those Park Rangers who wish to use the private Jefferson's views on religion to subvert the public arguments he made on religious liberty. The authors of *The Godless Constitution*, for example, draw no line between the public and the private Jefferson, lumping his private vitriol together with his public eloquence. They thus read Jefferson's private correspondence—words he explicitly requested be kept from public ears—into the text of the Virginia Bill for Establishing Religious Freedom and the U.S. Constitution itself. It is, in their words, "'coldly indifferent towards religion'—and a good thing, too." The result is a political theory that would tolerate scant display of religion in the public square—a religious liberty bent to fit a man who hated organized religion.

To grant them this argument is to grant them far too much. Allowing the public Jefferson's arguments on the nature of religious liberty to be undercut by the private Jefferson's misgivings about religion would be like amending "all men are created equal" to read "all men (except slaves) are created equal" because of Jefferson's flawed private views on slavery.

To be sure, Jefferson's motives in championing the cause of religious freedom were decidedly mixed. Whereas Madison believed that religious freedom would be good for religion, Jefferson apparently hoped it would be toxic to religion.

But, properly this time, so what? Neither Madison's more noble motives for advancing religious liberty nor Jefferson's cynical ones matter. What matters is the force of the public arguments they made. Just as Jefferson's personal views and failings don't rob the Declaration's argument of its intellectual force, so they don't detract from the public argument he actually made for religious liberty. Hypocrisy notwithstanding, he was right—all people *are* "created equal." They *are* endowed with "inalienable rights." And religious liberty *does* follow from the fact that "Almighty God hath created the mind free."

Madison and Jefferson disagreed on more than just *why* to protect the natural right to religious liberty. As we'll see in the next chapter, when it came time to ratify the Constitution they had a lively—and momentous—debate over *how* to protect it as well.

NINE

The Early First Amendment: A Disappointing Compromise

Reflections on Madison's greatest failure

Madison and Jefferson were arguing. Then again, nearly everybody in America was arguing. It was 1787 and the convention that had been called to amend the Articles of Confederation, America's first try at a constitution, had scrapped it instead and proposed an entirely new one. Had the delegates gone too far? Not far enough? And just who did they think they were anyway, proposing a new constitution?

Ratification was anything but certain. Many supported the new constitution; many opposed it. Those in the middle tended to be suspicious of it—especially since it lacked a bill of rights. That was Jefferson's main point. Writing to Madison from Paris, he listed the shortcomings he saw in the proposed constitution. "First," he said, was "the omission of a bill of rights providing clearly and without the aid of sophisms for freedom of religion, freedom of the press," and other rights. A bill of rights, Jefferson said, "is what people are entitled to against every government on earth." In short, for Jefferson, natural rights deserved legal protection.

There followed a lively back-and-forth in which an adamant Jefferson sought to persuade a skeptical Madison of the usefulness of a bill of rights. It's not that Madison didn't believe in rights. On the contrary, as we've seen, he was a champion of them. His objection was to codifying rights. He had very little faith in the power of what he called "parchment barriers" to contain popular sentiment. "Repeated violations of these parchment barriers," he observed, "have been committed by over-bearing majorities in every State." He saw no reason to suppose things would be any better at the federal level.

In fact, Madison saw a danger in the mere *attempt* to write down a set of rights for inclusion in the Constitution. As he explained to Jefferson, he was "sure that the rights of Conscience in particular, if submitted to public definition, would be narrowed much more than they are ever likely to be by an assumed power." For evidence, he pointed to the Puritans, who were upset that the new Constitution *lacked* a religious test for public office. "One of the objections in New England," Madison noted, "was that the Constitution by prohibiting religious tests opened a door for Jews, Turks, & infidels." If the question of religious liberty were to be run through the legislative sausage grinder, what would emerge might well be nauseating. A declaration of religious liberty, he concluded, "could not be obtained in the requisite latitude." Natural rights, for Madison, were too important to risk codifying them inadequately.

Jefferson replied pragmatically. Madison had a point, he said, but "half a loaf is better than no bread. If we cannot secure all our rights, let us secure what we can."

As we'll see, Madison gave in. And half a loaf is about all he got. America under the Articles of Confederation had been a patchwork of state-supported religions. What did it look like after the new Constitution was ratified? A patchwork of state-supported religions. And after the First Amendment was added, what did it look like then? Well, actually, it looked like a patchwork of state-supported religions.

It's a disappointing story. But one with an important lesson: either you take natural rights seriously or you don't. Paying them lip service while at the same time trading them off in a political compromise leads, at best, to a dulling of the national conscience. At worst, it leads to persecution. As we will see in coming chapters, that's exactly what developed. But let's not get ahead of ourselves. We'll take our disappointments one at a time.

First, some background.

Religion and the States...Take One:
The Articles of Confederation

The Articles of Confederation had been positively hair-raising on the subject of religion. The Articles not only assumed that the states would continue to maintain official religions, they even assumed there would be European-style wars of religion on American soil. Thus, Article III provided that a *war* prosecuted against one state, "*on account of religion,* sovereignty, trade, or any other pretense whatever," would be repelled by all other states. (Emphasis added.) So not only were wars of religion thinkable in America, they were thought to be worth fighting. Pluralism? The best that the Articles could do was implicitly demand that, in the event of a religious war launched against one state, other states with different official religions must still come to its aid.

That situation continued up through the Constitutional Convention of 1787. Some state constitutions affirmatively established religions. Massachusetts' constitution of 1780 is a good example:

> the legislature shall, from time to time, authorize and require, the several towns, parishes, precincts, and other bodies politic, or religious societies, to make suitable provision, at their own expense, for the institution of the public worship of God, and for the support and maintenance of public Protestant teachers of piety, religion and morality, in all cases where such provision shall not be made voluntarily.

Even more states—eleven out of thirteen—imposed religious tests for public office. Roger Williams' Rhode Island allowed only Protestants to vote or hold office, as did New Jersey, New Hampshire, North and South Carolina, Georgia and Vermont. Maryland and Massachusetts required merely a belief in the Christian religion, but William Penn's Pennsylvania required that office-holders be Protestants, believers in God and in the divine inspiration of both the Old and the New Testament. Delaware, in addition, went so far as to require profession of "faith in God the Father, and in Jesus Christ His only son, and in the Holy Ghost, one God blessed forevermore." The only states without religious tests were Virginia and New York.

Religion and the States... Take Two: The Unamended Constitution

Most Americans seem to think our Constitution changed all that. In fact, it didn't change much of anything. The Constitution left religious affairs in the states pretty much the way it found them. The only explicit mention of religion in the original, unamended Constitution was Article VI, section 3, which provided that officials of "*both* the United States *and* the several States" were to be "bound by Oath or Affirmation" to support the Constitution, and that "no religious test shall ever be required as a Qualification to any Office or public Trust *under the United States.*" (Emphasis added.) This was remarkable for two reasons. First, it accommodated the consciences of Quakers by providing that an affirmation was as good as an oath. Second, it is remarkable for the distinction it makes. Officials of both the federal government and the state governments were free to affirm instead of swear their support for the federal Constitution, but the prohibition on religious tests extended only to federal officials. Why? Because, as we've just seen, the overwhelming majority of states had their own religious tests for office and wanted to keep them. It was one thing to require the federal government to forgo religious tests; it was quite another to try to make the states forgo theirs. It wasn't religious tests that the framers opposed; it was *federal* religious tests (and a minority weren't opposed even to these). For most of the framers it went without saying that the legislature should be enforcing religious truth. They just wanted to make sure it was *their* legislature that was enforcing *their* religion, not the federal legislature enforcing somebody else's. In short, the unamended Constitution changed very little about religion in the states.

Religion and the States... Take Three: The Early First Amendment

The First Amendment didn't change much, either. Unfortunately, it too left the relationship between religion and state government exactly as it found it. That's because the story of religion in the First Amendment is largely the story of James Madison's compromises. It begins with a compromise on whether any religion amendment at all was a good idea. It ends with a fateful compromise on what such an amendment would protect—a compromise that was probably politically inevitable but that haunts us still.

A Conversion, of Sorts

Despite his misgivings, Madison switched sides and began supporting a bill of rights. Part of his motivation was political self-interest. In 1788, Madison was running for Congress and he had a problem. His old rival, Patrick Henry, was trying to defeat him by gerrymandering Madison's district to include a large number of Baptists, who were suspicious of Madison's reputed opposition to a bill of rights. So Madison made a campaign promise: Writing to a prominent Baptist minister, the Reverend John Leland, he explained that he now favored amendments to the Constitution to achieve "the most satisfactory provision for all essential rights, particularly the rights of Conscience in the fullest latitude." Madison made similar overtures to other Baptist ministers and was elected to Congress by 336 votes.

Madison had become convinced that proposing a bill of rights would be a shrewd strategy for more than just his congressional campaign. It would also be a good strategy for cementing widespread support for his Constitution generally. He was worried that a vocal minority of opponents would poison the new Constitution for everybody else. So he began to argue in Congress for a bill of rights, not so much because he thought it was a good idea for its own sake, as because he thought it was politically necessary. Many more people, he said, would get behind the new document if "only they could be satisfied on this one point."

What of his original worry that natural rights would be watered down in the process? He seems to have convinced himself that diluted rights could become more potent over time.

"The political truths declared in that solemn manner [i.e., in a bill of rights]," he wrote Jefferson, "acquire by degrees the character of fundamental maxims of free government." In short, he convinced himself he could gamble on a compromise.

He lost. Just as he had found in his work on the Virginia Declaration of Rights, when it came to the subject of rights, most of his fellow legislators agreed with him in principle more than in practice.

On the question of religious liberty, Madison proposed inserting language in the Constitution saying that "No State shall violate the equal rights of conscience, or the freedom of the press, or the trial by jury in criminal cases." The Senate, however, rejected this proposal. He also made a bid to abolish established churches in the states by submitting a draft that stated, "no religion shall be established by law." Others in the House of Representatives, however, feared (correctly) that this would lead to the abolition of the states' established churches.

Half a Loaf, Coming Right Up

Eventually, after a conference between the House and the Senate, the final text emerged. It was a major disappointment. "Congress," it read, "shall make no law respecting an establishment of religion, or prohibiting the free exercise thereof." Established religions would continue under the various state governments, though the federal government had no power either to establish its own religion or to disestablish that of a particular state. Massachusetts could keep its official religion, free from the fear that the federal government might try to abolish it. Virginia could keep its *dis*establishment, without worry that the federal government might try to impose its own official religion. Only states could establish or disestablish religions; Congress could do neither. It therefore could "make no law *respecting* an establishment of religion" (emphasis added).

The free exercise guarantee was likewise a disappointment. It too applied only to the federal government, not to the states. In 1842, for example, New Orleans fined a Roman Catholic priest named Father Permoli $50 for violating a city ordinance by performing a funeral rite in which the corpse was displayed in public. Father Permoli resisted the fine, arguing that it violated his right to free exercise of religion as protected by the First Amendment. The Supreme Court, however, held that "The Constitution makes no provision for protecting the citizens of the respective States in their religious liberties; this is left to the State Constitutions and laws: nor is there any inhibition imposed by the Constitution of the United States."

What's more, even against the federal government, the free exercise clause turned out to be a paper tiger. On its face, it forbade Congress from prohibiting the "free exercise" of religion. And free exercise was an idea with a fine reputation. It had been what George Calvert's marriage treaty had guaranteed Princess Henrietta Maria in the midst of a religiously tumultuous England; it had been what his Maryland Colony guaranteed at least most of its citizens. And it had been what Madison replaced the concept of tolerance with in the Virginia Declaration of Rights. It was his shorthand term for the natural right to religious liberty.

Unfortunately, the first big opportunity that the Supreme Court had to interpret "free exercise" came up in a case concerning Mormon polygamy in the federal territory of Utah. And just as "hard cases make bad law" and "great cases make bad law," so too bigamy cases make bad law.

In the 1860s, Mormon settlers were streaming into Utah Territory, where they could be free from persecution. At the time, polygamy was still an accepted practice of the Mormon Church, but not at all an accepted practice of the United States. Congress had passed a law making polygamy a crime in the territories, and a man named George Reynolds was convicted of the offense. Reynolds had an interesting defense: he freely admitted to having two wives, but claimed that the free exercise clause gave him the right to do so. The Supreme Court disagreed, ruling that free exercise was no defense for violating a duly enacted law.

Now, if all the Court had ruled was that the Mormons' right to free exercise had to yield to the government's overwhelming interest in defending traditional marriage, the case would have been largely unremarkable. But the Court went far beyond that. In fact, in its rush to weed out polygamy, the Court managed to uproot much of the meaning of free exercise. According to the chief justice, "Laws are made for the government of actions, and while they cannot interfere with mere religious belief and opinions, they may with practices." The free exercise clause thus meant only that Congress had no power over private beliefs, but was free to punish public actions. Some right. You can think all you want, you just can't act on your thoughts. If this doesn't sound terribly free (or, for that matter, much like exercise) anymore, that's because it wasn't.

What about the Other Half?

When it came to religion, the Bill of Rights was thus barely a bill of rights at all. The establishment clause was essentially a states' rights provision. And the right to free exercise wasn't broadly guaranteed. As interpreted by the Supreme Court, it protected little more than the right to believe—and even this was protected only against federal incursions, not those by the states. On the contrary, the First Amendment implicitly recognized the *legitimacy* of state interference with free exercise and the *legitimacy* of state-established religions. The First Amendment was, as Jefferson said and Madison feared, "half a loaf."

Reflecting later in life, Madison apparently still thought so. He continued to distinguish between the Constitution's protections and "pure...religious freedom." In a rambling treatise that has been dubbed his "detached memorandum," Madison criticized the government-funded appointment of congressional chaplains. (He thereby staked out a position that even the modern Supreme Court has rejected, but that must have reminded the elderly Madison of the battles of his youth in the Virginia legislature.) In doing so, he asked rhetorically whether it was "consistent with the Constitution, *and with the pure principle of religious freedom?*" "In strictness," he said, "the answer *on both points* must be in the negative." (Emphasis added.) He then went on to make a textual argument under the First Amendment and an "equal rights" argument under the "pure principle." Madison obviously didn't believe that the existence of the Constitution somehow superseded the natural rights that it imperfectly echoed. So even though the First Amendment was not all he believed it should be, all was not lost. There were still natural rights to which we could appeal.

All may not have been lost, but much was severely damaged. Not only did persecution remain legal in the states, but the citizenry went on believing that states could legitimately outlaw or establish religions at will at the same time they heard the rhetoric of natural rights. George Washington, for example, wrote a famous letter to the Touro Synagogue in 1790. Referring to religious liberty, he said, "It is now no more that toleration is spoken of, as if it was by the indulgence of one class of people, that another enjoyed the exercise of their inherent natural rights." But as we'll see in the next chapter, Jews actually enjoyed precious few of their "inherent natural rights." Left free to persecute, most states wrote anti-Semitism directly into their laws, if not into their state constitutions. Washington was right. Toleration was no longer "spoken of"; natural rights were. That was the problem: Natural rights were spoken of, not protected; toleration wasn't spoken of, but continued in practice. And that combination soon proved toxic to religious liberty.

TEN

In the States, the Aftermath of Compromise

Reflections on legalized persecution under the early First Amendment

It was May 1844, and Philadelphia was burning. It all began when one group staged a demonstration in the Kensington area of the city, the stronghold of its opponents. A fight broke out. Then there was a shot, and soon a riot. Later that night the demonstrators tried to set fire to a building, only to be repulsed by a makeshift militia bent on defending it. Things quickly escalated. A mass rally was called, speeches were made, and both sides were soon enraged. Within days, several schools, along with many homes and churches, had been burned.

Schools?

Catholic schools, to be precise. The demonstrators were so-called "Nativist" Protestants, a popular movement that identified being Protestant with being American. Their opponents were mostly immigrant Irish Catholics. And the demonstrations in Kensington had been in favor of keeping in place the law that required all schoolchildren to read the Protestant version of the Bible in public schools. Burning down the only available alternative—Catholic schools—had a certain ruthless logic to it. Setting fire to Catholic churches and homes reinforced the message.

There were religious riots elsewhere as well, notably in Manhattan. The issue was the same. To the Nativists, Catholics couldn't be truly American because they were loyal to the pope, a "foreign prince," and—what's beyond irony—because they were hostile to the idea of religious liberty. Their mass immigration was therefore thought to be a disaster that could be mitigated only by a concerted effort to reprogram their children as good American Protestants. It was important, then, that as many of the little immigrants as possible be sent to public schools, and imperative that those public schools enforce at least a lowest-common-denominator Protestantism. For the Nativists, keeping the Bible—the *King James* Bible—legally required in public schools was well worth a riot or two. And, as we'll see, when the Nativists gained political power they unleashed some truly rabid anti-Catholic legislation.

It wasn't just anti-Catholicism, though. Far from it. Anti-Semitism was positively endemic—and shockingly explicit. Quakers, as we've seen, were oppressed almost everywhere. Other religious minorities fared badly too. Madison had feared this would happen. He had warned Jefferson of the fickleness of the individual states, which paid lip service to the idea of natural rights but legislated as if no one had ever heard of them. The story of the minority religions in the states shows just how right he was—and how big a mistake the First Congress made when it rejected his version of the First Amendment and instead chose one that didn't apply to the states.

That compromise had left the states free to continue their own official religions as well as to deny free exercise to minority faiths. Where did it lead? To persecution, yes. But also to confusion. Pronouncing loudly that there is a natural right to religious freedom, then saying that the states could continue to persecute, resulted in cognitive dissonance, to say the least.

The story thus poses a question: After the First Amendment had been ratified and had left the states legally free to persecute religious minorities, were the states morally free to persecute them as well? If the law says we *can* be anti-Catholic or anti-Semitic, *may* we be? And if not, why not?

Members Only: Legal Anti-Catholicism

Nativism wasn't confined to school-burning extremists. Whole political movements sprang up expressly devoted to the cause of keeping America Protestant. The most successful was the American Party, also known as the "Know-Nothing" party.

The Know-Nothings took their name from the first-degree ritual of something called the Order of the Star-Spangled Banner, in which the initiates would swear, among other things, not to disclose anything about the organization, if necessary even denying its existence. If asked whether he knew anything about the order, a member would have to claim to "know nothing." More to the point, he would also swear to "vote only for native born American citizens...to the exclusion of all...Roman-Catholics."

The Know-Nothings' greatest success came in Massachusetts. In 1854 they won the governorship, the entire congressional delegation, all forty seats in the Massachusetts Senate, and all but three of the 379 members of the state's House of Representatives. They then proceeded to require reading of the King James Bible in all common schools; to propose constitutional amendments that would have "deprived Roman Catholics of their right to hold public office and restricted office and the suffrage to male citizens who had resided in the country for no less than twenty-one years"; to dismiss Irish government employees; and to ban foreign-language instruction in the schools. They even established a "Joint Special Committee on the Inspection of Nunneries and Convents." (Much to their disappointment, no dungeons were uncovered.)

Abraham Lincoln once said of the Know-Nothings: "As a nation we began by declaring that 'all men are created equal.' We now practically read it 'all men are created equal, except Negroes.' When the Know-Nothings get control, it will read 'all men are created equal except Negroes and foreigners and Catholics.' When it comes to this, I shall prefer emigrating to some country where they make no pretence of loving liberty."

The Know-Nothings' most lasting legacy was the passage of "Blaine Amendments" in states around the country. These were amendments to state constitutions that prohibited public funds from being distributed to "sectarian" schools, or schools run by religious "sects." The Massachusetts Know-Nothings' version provided that "Moneys raised by taxation in the towns and cities for the support of public schools, and all moneys which may be appropriated by the state for the support of common schools...shall never be appropriated to any religious sect for the maintenance exclusively of its own schools." Over half the states now have amendments similar to this one.

Note that Blaine Amendments didn't prohibit money from going to *religious* schools; they only prohibited money from gong to *sectarian* ones. That's because Blaine Amendments were not designed to keep religion *out* of the public schools. Rather, they were part of a program to keep a particular sort of religion *in* them—and make it expensive for immigrant Catholics to go elsewhere. Blaine Amendments were designed to protect the hegemony of the so-called common (i.e., public) schools, which taught the so-called common (i.e., Protestant) religion. Catholicism was a "sect" because it wouldn't subscribe to that "common religion."

Blaine Amendments take their name from an opportunistic bigot named James G. Blaine. He was Speaker of the House in the U.S. Congress in 1875 and almost succeeded in advancing a similar amendment to the United States Constitution. It passed the House 380-3, but failed in the Senate. In truth, however, as Massachusetts shows, Blaine was just trying to capitalize on what the Know-Nothings had accomplished over the previous quarter-century. He did not fail completely. In subsequent years, his followers were able to muster a majority to require that Blaine Amendments be added to new states' constitutions as a condition of their being admitted to the Union.

Directly and indirectly, the Know-Nothings accomplished much. Perhaps their greatest success, though, is this: Even today, a century and a half since they began their drive to enshrine bigotry in American law, most people still know nothing of who they were or the legacy they left.

Nor do most people know our shameful history of legalized anti-Semitism.

Rounding Up the Usual Suspects: Legalized Anti-Semitism

General Order no. 11: "The Jews, as a class...are hereby expelled from this department within twenty-four hours from the receipt of this order by post commanders. They will see that this class of people are furnished with passes and required to leave; and any one returning after such notification, will be arrested and held in confinement until an opportunity occurs of sending them out as prisoners...."

Germany, 1939, right? Guess again.

United States, 1862. At the height of the Civil War, a Union general decided to crack down on smuggling. He used the Jewish community as a scapegoat for what were actually widespread trade violations, forcing Jews out of their homes with no chance to protest and no opportunity to protect their livelihoods. The "department" referred to was the so-called Department of Tennessee, the Union-occupied war zone. And the general was none other than Ulysses S. Grant.

The order caused an immediate outcry. Cesar Kaskel, one of the Jews displaced under the order, fired off telegrams, notified the press, and traveled immediately to Washington, where he made a personal plea before President Lincoln. The president wasted no time in responding, forcing the secretary of war to revoke the order. A prominent Jewish organization then sent its thanks to the president and the secretary for revoking "this illegal, unjust, and tyrannical mandate, depriving American citizens of the Jewish faith, of their precious rights."

Their precious *natural* rights, certainly. But what, exactly, were their rights *legally*? It wasn't an easy question to answer. They varied in quality from state to state (ranging generally between bad and worse). They varied sharply between Lincoln's relative protection of Jews from *federal* oppression and his— and every other federal official's—legal impotence to protect them from *state* oppression.

Jews were the object of distrust and apprehension from the time they first arrived in America. Political leaders who couldn't tolerate dissident Christians were hardly prepared to accept non-Christians. The Constitution had done little to alleviate the problem: the states still held power over religion, and they could create any restrictions they saw fit.

And they saw fit. Most states barred Jews from holding public office; a few went even further. Take, for instance, Maryland. Even on its best days, colonial Maryland had refused to extend toleration to Jews. Things were little better under the federal Constitution. By 1797, the Constitution of Maryland denied Jews not only the right to hold elected office, but the right to hold *any* civil position, fight in the militia, or practice law. Proponents of religious liberty introduced a bill that would extend to Jews "the same civil privileges that are enjoyed by other religious sects." Despite the relatively small number of Jews in the state, the so-called "Jew bill" became a hot issue in Maryland politics. The major proponent of the bill—a young Presbyterian legislator with no Jews in his district, but a fervent belief in religious liberty—was voted out of office after being labeled "an enemy of Christianity" and "Judas Iscariot." When the bill first appeared in 1802, the legislature (no surprise) promptly voted it down. It was voted down again in 1819, and again in 1823. It was not until 1825 that the law gathered sufficient support, and the following year Jews were finally granted full political rights in the state.

Progress in Maryland was practically speedy compared with that in other states. When Connecticut wrote its constitution in 1818, it abolished the longstanding established church, and even went so far as to declare equal "powers, rights, and privileges" for "every society or denomination of Christians in this state." But equality was still for Christians. Jews need not apply. The same was true in New Hampshire, which did not allow Jews (or Catholics, for that matter) to hold office until 1876. Jews faced similar uphill battles in North Carolina and Massachusetts. In fact, they did not gain full political rights in all states until 1877.

Some states were more equal-opportunity oppressors, their opprobrium falling on (among others) Jews, Catholics and atheists alike. Their instrument of choice was the test oath. Vermont's is a restrictive, but not unusual, example: "You do believe in one God, the Creator and Governor of the Universe, the rewarder of the good, and punisher of the wicked. And you do acknowledge the scriptures of the Old and New Testament to be given by divine inspiration; and own and profess the Protestant religion." These states were perfectly willing to grant you freedom of religion: you were free to be any kind of Protestant you wanted.

Starting Again, from the Beginning

So much for the story. Now the question: Was it any less wrong for a Vermont official to persecute Jews and Catholics than it was for General Grant to attempt to expel Jews from Tennessee? And if it was just as wrong, why was it just as wrong? Once again, it can't be because state-law persecution was unconstitutional—it wasn't unconstitutional then; the First Amendment didn't yet apply to the states. And it wasn't illegal. Anti-Semitism and anti-Catholicism, for example, were both legally required in Vermont. So what was wrong about it? Put differently, when the federal Constitution left the states free to continue their religious persecutions and the states enacted those persecutions into law, were the Jews, Catholics and other minorities without religious liberty? Or was their religious liberty being violated?

It all depends on where religious freedom comes from. If religious liberty comes from the state, then nineteenth-century Jews and Catholics in Vermont had none because the state didn't choose to give them any and the federal government wouldn't protect them. If, on the other hand, religious liberty is a moral limitation imposed on the state, then Vermont might violate it but could never repeal or amend it, no matter what the Vermont Constitution said. And the federal Constitution's compromise may have left religious freedom legally unprotected but couldn't have eliminated it, either.

If that's the case, though, our current interpretation of the First Amendment can't be the last word on religious liberty any more than the nineteenth century's interpretation was.

It is time, then, to ask where religious liberty comes from, what its contours are, and how we know. We can no longer settle for asking what James Madison or Roger Williams *thought* about these questions, as if this were just an exercise in historical analysis. Nor can we content ourselves with wondering how most Supreme Court justices might vote on them this week, as if this were merely a legal matter. Rather, we must ask these questions for ourselves, in our own voice.

A tall task? Yes, but fortunately we have help: a six-year-old Buddhist little boy whom we'll meet in the next chapter.

Part Three

Authentic Freedom

Where Does Religious Liberty Come From?

Reflections on who we are to deserve freedom

He was six years old when they arrested him in 1995. Assuming he's still living, he has now spent ten years in custody. And it is quite likely he will remain in custody for the rest of his life.

What crime could a six-year-old boy possibly commit that would warrant a life sentence? None. Gedhun Choekyi Nyima is not even alleged to have committed any crime at all. The Chinese government has kept him in custody not because he's a criminal. He's not. He is being held solely because Tibetan Buddhists believe him to be the reincarnation of a major religious figure known as the Panchen Lama—someone second only to the Dalai Lama in their hierarchy—and Chinese officials fear anybody they don't control.

For the past decade our State Department has been denouncing Gedhun's detention as an outrage against religious liberty. The Chinese response has always been the same—that our protests are an improper interference in their internal affairs. They are adamant: under Chinese law, the decision to detain one of their citizens, whether six years old or sixty, for any reason or no reason, is theirs to make. Period.

Now, why aren't they right?

Mary and Gedhun

That question—why aren't they right?—is just another version of the question we asked at the end of Chapter Four: why didn't

Mary Dyer have it coming? Recall that Mary Dyer was legally hanged on Boston Common for preaching against the Massachusetts Bay Colony. She had insisted on returning from exile to preach against the colony even after having been warned that the legislature had enacted the death penalty for returning Quakers like her. Her execution was the low point of religious liberty in America. Yet why wasn't it proper? Hanging her wasn't illegal—it was legally required. It wasn't unconstitutional—there wasn't a constitution yet. The duly elected authorities had duly enacted the law under which she was hanged. She had notice of the law and chose to violate it. And she was duly arrested and tried for her offense. Why shouldn't she hang? Why didn't she have it coming?

And that question itself is just another version of the one we asked at the end of the last chapter: Why wasn't it proper for state governments to persecute Jews, Catholics and other minorities in the eighteenth, nineteenth and early twentieth centuries? After all, the federal Constitution permitted it then and state law required it.

So, why didn't Mary Dyer have it coming, why wasn't legalized anti-Semitism proper, and why aren't the Chinese right today?

The short answer is, because liberty is a human right, not just a constitutional one. It isn't some legal nicety, but a universal moral limit on the government's power. It doesn't come from Chinese law in the first place, so Chinese law, while it may *violate* religious freedom, can never really repeal it. Religious liberty is as much a human right in China as it is here, regardless of what China's law says.

But this works both ways. If religious liberty truly is universal, then it must also be as much a human right *here* as it is anywhere else—regardless of what our law says. Recall the provision in Thomas Jefferson's Bill for Establishing Religious Freedom that warned against future attempts at repealing or narrowing it. While it conceded that nothing could stop future legislatures from tampering with its protections, the bill went on to warn "that the rights hereby asserted are of the *natural rights of mankind*, and that if any act shall be hereafter passed to repeal the present, or to narrow its operation, such act will be *an infringement of natural right.*" (Emphasis added.) In other words, while no law can force legislators once and for all to recognize the moral limits to their power, those moral limits remain nonetheless. They may be violated but they can't be eliminated.

The long answer requires us to begin at the beginning, to ask why there should be religious liberty at all, what it protects and how we know.

So Then, Where Does It Come From?

If we take seriously the idea that religious liberty is a universal human right, a right possessed by people everywhere, then we must seek its origins not in things that change but in things that don't. It can't be based on something like law, which is liable to vary radically over time or across cultures; otherwise it would vary radically, too. It wouldn't be universal. No, universal human rights must be based on something universally human. And vague appeals to "human nature" won't suffice. To grasp the contours of religious liberty we must understand precisely what it is about our common humanity that gives rise to it. As we've learned from Jefferson's appalling shortcomings on slavery, it's important not to skip this step. In short, if religious liberty is a right that is valid always and everywhere, it must follow from specific traits that are typically human always and everywhere.

It must follow, in other words, from a universal human *truth.* (Cue scary music.) Yet the truth is nothing to fear; it's no threat to freedom. Universal human rights are secured, not threatened, by grounding them in this sort of truth claim. To quote Jefferson on one of his good days, it's "a *truth*...that the exercise of religion should be *free.*"

Human rights are all the more broadly secured when they're grounded in this sort of *human* truth claim. As we've learned from Roger Williams' mistake in Rhode Island, saying that people have religious liberty because God told you so convinces only the people who believe that God talks to you. Not even as noble a claim as the Jewish and Christian one that all are created in the image and likeness of God will be convincing to someone outside those traditions. By contrast, grounding religious liberty in observable traits in our common humanity makes it a right recognizable by people from all traditions or from no tradition at all. People who disagree on who God is (or even if God is) can nevertheless agree on who we are. And that means they can agree on the nature and scope of a religious liberty based on our common humanity.

So, who are we, anyway, that we have religious liberty?

Born Free—and Smart

We are persons. That is, we're intelligent and free beings who are naturally able to know and to choose—and who are naturally urged by our consciences to choose well. We're each unique; but we're not isolated, lonely little hermits. While our lives are our own, we naturally want to live them in community with others, expressing freely all that's important to us. The experience of these things is universal; it cuts across cultural boundaries. And it therefore points up a right that is universal, that itself cuts across cultural boundaries.

Now, let's unpack all that.

I Love You for My Mind

We are intelligent beings; we want to *know*. What do we want to know? Once again, the truth—about anything and everything. From childhood on, we want to understand what makes things tick. (Just try to get a three-year-old to stop asking "Why?") We may be curious about different subjects, but we are characteristically curious nonetheless. We want the facts. And we want them to be accurate. Whether we're reading batting averages, annual reports or scientific data, we won't tolerate made-up numbers. There's simply no point in reading statistics if the numbers aren't right. Put differently, there's no point in reading them unless the numbers are *true*. Even in situations where we have to settle for some sort of estimate, we immediately wonder how we can improve on it. Our minds are very demanding: only the truth will ultimately satisfy them.

The thing is, there's never quite enough truth to slake our thirst for it. It seems there's always something more that we just have to know. Every new truth we discover leads us to pose new questions.

What's more, our need for truth doesn't stop with small or easy-to-measure things. We also crave the truth about other sorts of things, things that are bigger and harder to measure. Questions such as, "Do I love her?" and, "Does she love me?" are important ones. And they have true answers, even if they're answers that are hard to find. The biggest questions of life—is there a God, who is He and what does He want of me—are like that, too. Very hard, very important. For that matter, even the truth closest to home—who we are—is like that. As Nietzsche put it, "We are unknown to ourselves, we knowers...." Our existence, and the fact that we obviously didn't create ourselves, pose a famous series of questions: "Who are we, where did we come from, and where are we going?" None of these important truths comes cheap. To find them, even partially, we must decisively seek them. And that search is often consuming. People have found through the centuries and across cultures, though, that it's a price they're willing to pay. Every society has its philosophers, its poets, its priests or its druids. They search on because they simply need to know. And on a less professional, more everyday level, so do we.

What's more, when we reflect on it, we consider the search for truth an adventure, not a chore. That's because truth is more than just information about other good things—it's a good thing itself. It's something we want for its own sake. Mark Twain once defined a classic as "a book everyone wants to have read but no one wants to read." Every undergraduate knows the experience. Truth isn't like that for us. We don't want to have learned it just so we can get on with life. We enjoy discovering it. It's something that tastes good all by itself.

And now that we mention taste...

Choose Well—Choose Good

While our minds are busy looking for truth, our hearts (or, in classical terms, our "wills") are off in search of the good life. They're constantly on the lookout for good things and they're constantly selecting among them. Our wills are what we shop with.

Now, there are goods and there are goods. We're naturally hungry for all sorts of things, from the mundane to the exquisite. On the one hand, we have a big appetite for everyday sorts of goods—from food to clothes to cars. And it's an appetite that's never really satisfied. Sometimes it's a desire for excellence; sometimes it's just greed. But we're never quite content with what we have. We don't just want more stuff either; we want better stuff. As the bumper sticker says, "Life's too short to drink bad wine." We're constantly questing for the perfect lawn, the ultimate golf ball, a light beer that doesn't taste like one.

On the other hand, our hearts have a different sort of hunger for more noble goods. We seek beauty and joy, friendship and family; we want to love and to be loved. Once again, though, we're never quite satisfied. Art lovers don't love only a single painting. Nobody wants just one friend. The same is true with the quality of such things. We don't just want more art; we want better art. We don't just want more friendships; we want deeper ones. No matter how ordinary or how sublime the good, we just can't get enough.

Now, how do we manage all this? How do we deal with our various, often conflicting, sometimes tumultuous desires? We're faced with decisions a hundred times a day. How is it that we're not paralyzed before them? Or why aren't we doomed to randomly chase one thing after another? Put differently, what enables us to give our lives direction by making meaningful decisions?

Our capacity to choose. Our willpower and our minds and emotions give us the ability to make choices and stick with them. They turn our lives into projects. They make us free. Writ large, our ability to choose freely is what enables the Sakharovs and Mandelas and Walesas of the world to reject tyranny whatever the cost. Writ small, it's what enables us to obey the alarm clock and get out of bed despite how good it feels to stay.

Our built-in desire for good and our freedom to choose are undeniably universal. Anyone who doesn't want good things, who seeks instead to inflict random pain and deprivation on himself or herself, we consider clinically diagnosable. Likewise, those who don't feel free to choose we call obsessive/compulsive. The normal, typically human thing is to be constantly on the lookout for ever-better things and to freely choose among them.

Listen Up

We soon discover, though, that our choices have consequences. True, our lives are our projects; we can make of them what we will. We find, however, that not only are we free to mold our lives by our choices, but also that we must mold them well if we're to be happy and fulfilled. It seems obvious to us, if a little frightening, that our choices constitute us as persons. By freely choosing what is good or what is evil (though it always seems so good at the time), we freely become good or evil. How do we choose? How can we tell the good from the evil? In facing these questions we experience our capacity to judge, as well as an insistent urge to obey those judgments. We experience, in other words, our conscience.

Conscience is what lives at the crossroads where the questing, restless human intellect meets the free and hungry human will. We experience it as something of a mystery: it's clearly part of us, yet seems curiously distinct; its judgments are our own judgments and yet we find that we must obey them. Conscience isn't so much a scold (though it can be fearsome when crossed) as it is a demanding mentor. It's the interior voice that requires the best of us, insisting that we seek what's true and choose what's good in the concrete circumstances of life.

Our minds and wills give us an inherent nobility. They give us a built-in desire to know the truth and taste the good; they make us able to think and choose for ourselves. But conscience ensures that, in Shakespeare's words, "Uneasy lies the head that wears the crown." Conscience won't let us be satisfied with resting on the truth we already know, the good we already embrace. There is an unease we experience, an unease that pushes us on to seek ever-deeper truths and choose ever-better goods. Sometimes we ignore it; sometimes we try to suppress it. Conscience, however, demands that we attend to it and miss no opportunity to try to satisfy it. Conscience is forever insisting that we look here, or search there, or try this or that in our quest for the true and the good.

And then conscience still isn't content. It won't stand for the argument that searching alone should suffice. Conscience demands not only that we seek but that we embrace the truth we believe we've found. It insists that, at whatever cost, our convictions follow through into action. And it's famously stubborn about this, sending generation after generation of dissidents to all sorts of deprivations in the name of integrity. That meant, for the Quakers, preaching though the government forbade it, declining oaths though the government required them, and refusing military service though the government ordered it.

Why couldn't the Quakers just stay home and keep their ideas to themselves? Why did they have to be so divisive? For the same reason dissidents have always refused to be silenced: conscience. They were convinced that they knew an important truth that was being overlooked or denied by the powers-that-be. Their consciences wouldn't let them rest until they sounded the alarm. And conscience came first.

Conscience is universally recognized as quintessentially human. Even those who lack the courage to follow their own consciences into adversity revere the heroes who do.

So, Why Religious Liberty?

We are, then, a community of conscientious truth-seekers and good-lovers. So it's only natural that we each hope—in fact, are driven—to find an ultimate truth and an exquisite good that will quench our thirst. To be human is to long for a truth desired, maybe even half-remembered, but not fully grasped. It's to yearn for a satisfying good, one that lies far beyond the horizon of ourselves. We sense that we're somehow incomplete without that truth, unfailingly thirsty without that good, and we long to find it. True, we may break off consciously searching from time to time, or try to suppress our longing. But the experiences of life usually drive us back to it, as we seek to understand why we suffer, who and what we should love, whether there is anything worth dying for. At least in the back of our minds, we're constantly on the lookout for an ultimate truth and a surpassing good. For God, in other words.

We're at our best when we're searching for God. The deepest aspects of our humanity are all fully engaged: our truth-seeking minds are chasing the deepest truth there could be; our good-loving wills are after the best good imaginable; and our consciences are happy, and insistent, about the whole thing. Searching for God is a thoroughly human thing to do.

But only when it's free. A mind that's seeking the ultimate truth can't with integrity settle for something unconvincing just because it's being pressured. No matter how transcendent the truth, forcing it on people violates their dignity as intelligent beings. Likewise, the notion of a "forced free will" makes no sense—especially when what that will is freely doing is looking for the ultimate good.

The decision to embrace an ultimate truth claim is like loving another person; it must be free if it's to be real. This is one of the facts of life, which generations of teenagers must learn again and again: You can't nag, cajole, badger or coerce someone into loving you. And if you do eventually bully or besiege the object of your affection until she or he sighs, "*Fine* then, I love you," the one thing you can be certain of is that the professed love isn't genuine. It's a surrender, not an embrace. In fact, not only will your campaign not have won you true love, it will have succeeded only in sullying the one you so strenuously seek—it will have coerced her into lying about something as important as love. It's the same with faith. To be coerced into professing it doesn't make us converts, but hypocrites.

In short, we have a conscience-driven, fundamental need for

religious search and expression. It is quintessentially human. And when something quintessentially human requires freedom in order to be authentic, it's wrong to rob it of its authenticity by robbing it of its freedom.

That's *why* religious liberty. Now, what is its scope?

The scope of our humanity. Because it arises from our minds' pursuit of truth, together with our consciences' insistence that we embrace the truth as we know it, religious liberty includes the right to seek the truth and lay claim to what it is we believe we've found. Because it arises from our hearts' quest for the good, together with our consciences' demand that we *do* good and avoid evil, religious liberty includes the right to conform our lives—within broad limits—to the good as we grasp it.

There is also a third aspect of religious liberty that we'll consider next, the social aspect. Coincidentally, we'll again have a six-year-old boy to help us. This one's name is Zach and nobody thinks he's the reincarnation of anyone. He's just a normal little boy—which is the whole point.

TWELVE

Personal, Not Private

Reflections on why believers do it in public

The previous afternoon, Zach's first-grade teacher had given him the big news. "Tomorrow," she had said, "you're going to read in front of the whole class for the first time." But that wasn't all. "Your reward," she had added, "is that you get to read from your favorite book."

So that morning Zach brought in his favorite book—his cartoon *Beginner's Bible,* and told his teacher that the story he had chosen to read to the class was the story of Jacob and Esau, which the *Beginner's Bible* dubbed "The Big Family." It didn't even mention God. Nevertheless, his teacher forbade Zach from reading that story, or anything else for that matter, from the *Beginner's Bible.* Zach couldn't read it to the class, she said, but had to read it to her separately and in private.

Zach was crushed. His mom, an artist who understood the importance of freedom of expression, was angry. She retained the Becket Fund and we went to war. Soon, Zach and his *Beginner's Bible* became something of a poster child for religious expression in public. He was featured on the *Today* show and on CNN, in *Newsweek,* the *Wall Street Journal* and the *Washington Post.* The U.S. Court of Appeals heard his case three times. The case finally settled when we got word that the U.S. Department of Education was issuing regulations cutting off the federal funding of any school district that did a similar thing in the future.

Zach's situation struck a nerve because it was both picturesque and touching. But it was also very typical of what happens in less picturesque, less touching ways every day: an officious Park Ranger—whether a public school teacher, a city council member or a judge—assumes that religious expression is proper only in private and so tries to squelch it in public.

We're Not Idiots

Even well-meaning Park Rangers who accept religious liberty as a human right assume that religion belongs only in private. "Fine," they say, "you need to search for the true and the good. All right. But why don't you just search away at home, and leave the rest of us out of it? Why do you have to do it in the streets and frighten the horses?"

Because our humanity, from which religious freedom comes, is bigger than just our minds and hearts. So while religious liberty may begin with the freedom to seek and embrace truth and goodness, it doesn't end there.

We aren't hermits, or even loners, grimly searching for truth and goodness with our eyes glued to the ground, ignoring one another. We're born instead with the desire for community. While each of us is unique, we humans are social creatures, eager to reach out and embrace not just some private truth, but other people around us. We naturally form families, gather in clans and tribes, display our arts, and commemorate with ritual the great events of life.

It's not that we *can't* live alone—we can. But typically we don't enjoy it. "Solitary" is one of our harshest punishments. And those who voluntarily shun other people are unflatteringly tagged as "recluses," or worse. This is not a recent development, either. Society has long stigmatized the self-absorbed. Our word "idiot," for example, derives from the Greek *idiotes*, which in ancient Athens referred to an excessively private person who didn't participate in the life of the community. Called by whatever name, however, withdrawing from society is simply not normal. We try not to live isolated lives because we find them distressing; it's not who we are.

What's more, we're not just social beings in the sense that we like a good party. It goes deeper than that. We're also social beings in the sense that we're cultural beings. We naturally want to live our lives in a larger context with others, to stand in a tradition. We don't enjoy having to make life up as we go along. In both space and time—that is, in the arts and in the rhythm of the calendar—we want to express and reinforce who we are: how we celebrate birth and mourn death, how we understand love and sexuality, what we're prepared to fight and die for, and so on. Culture tells the world—and reminds us—who we are.

Part of this is expressing what we believe. Just as the other quintessentially personal aspects of our lives have a cultural dimension, so does our faith. We don't believe in private because we don't live in private. This has always been the case. We believe so we daub paint on prehistoric cave walls, spend generations building cathedrals, sculpt the *David*, compose the *Messiah* and write *The Brothers Karamazov*. The personal thing to do is, and always has been, not to keep our beliefs private but to express them in culture.

And the Horses Aren't That Skittish

But wait, the Park Rangers insist, it was all so much simpler then. There was no problem what to put on the cave walls when everyone who lived in the cave believed in the same Cosmic Bull. But what if it had been then as it is now? What if some believed in a Cosmic Bull while others believed in a Cosmic Lion and still others thought they were both crazy? Wouldn't they have had to leave the cave walls bare just to keep from killing each other? And isn't that what we must do now?

No. That's the whole point: It's inhuman to leave the cave walls bare. (Even men's college dorm rooms have something on the walls.) We simply can't live without a culture. And we can't live happily without an authentic culture, either. That is, we can't live happily without a culture that reflects and expresses the full scope of our humanity. So just as it's inhuman to attempt to live without any culture at all, it's equally inhuman to say we can have a culture only so long as there's no religion—or love or sex or marriage or death—in it.

"Well, then, at least leave the government out of it" is the

Park Rangers' fallback position. "There are plenty of houses of worship that can host Nativity scenes and menorahs and so forth. Why do we need courthouse steps? After all, not everyone celebrates Hanukkah or Christmas." No, of course they don't. In a pluralistic society there's nothing that *everyone* celebrates. A minority of people celebrate St. Patrick's Day, for example, yet everyone else puts up with it. Anglophiles don't sue to block St. Patrick's Day Parades, just as European-Americans don't challenge African-American History Month. They have no reason to. The mayor can and does wear green on March 17 while taking no real position on the relative merits of being Irish. It's the same with Christmas and Hanukkah. The mayor can celebrate these, too, without taking a position on the mystery of the Incarnation or the miracle of the oils.

And he or she should. Whatever surface appeal the leave-the-government-out-of-it argument may have, things aren't that simple. It's impossible for the government to be silent on religion in culture because its silence itself speaks volumes. If the government were uninvolved in our culture generally, there would be no problem with it being uninvolved in our religious expression. But it's not uninvolved at all. The government is a major force in the culture. It celebrates everything from National Catfish Day to National Jukebox Week. It proclaims national holidays to commemorate a wide variety of things, from Thanksgiving to Memorial Day to Martin Luther King Day. It runs a comprehensive public school system that purports to teach children what they need to know about everything from literature to sex. It provides public universities that not only educate in the arts, but are a major venue for their performance and display, as well as a formidable intellectual force in the debate about them. And the government's reach extends even further. It actually underwrites the arts of its choosing. Taken together, the government-run educational system, its subsidy of the arts, its proclamation of holidays all combine to create a cultural force of seismic proportions.

For the government to play such a role, however, while never mentioning our spiritual dimension is very different from saying nothing on the subject. It is implicitly saying something profound—that religion is at best an unimportant, and at worst a shameful, aspect of our lives.

Put differently, if the government is to play such a significant role in the culture, it must be honest. While it may be the proper business of the government to elevate our culture—to underwrite classical music concerts that the market might not otherwise support, for example—it is not the business of the government to attempt to fundamentally redefine our self-understanding. When the government acknowledges the obvious—we human beings have a spiritual thirst and it is only natural for us to try to slake it—it is doing as it ought. Conversely, when it resolutely omits that aspect of our humanity, while otherwise offering a comprehensive culture, it does us a profound disservice. We not only suffer the opportunity cost of human truths unexpressed, but we actually are injured by the implicit lie that we are not spiritually inclined after all.

Now of course not every petty bureaucrat who bans a Christmas tree from his little bailiwick is a Pol Pot in the making. But he or she is a menace nonetheless. Meddlesome Park Ranger bureaucrats are in a very real sense public liars. By peddling a less-than-authentic culture—one that excludes our spiritual dimension—they lie to us about who we really are.

If, though, the Pilgrims are wrong to insist on only one religion in culture, and the Park Rangers are wrong to insist on no religion at all in culture, what's the alternative—all religions in culture? Yes. Not out of some theory of relativism, or an undifferentiated enthusiasm for diversity, but out of respect for consciences, mistaken and otherwise.

In a religiously diverse society, there are really only three options: First, the government can choose only one religion to recognize in culture. That is both illegal and immoral (not to mention dumb—what are the odds that the people who brought you the IRS and the DMV are going to get theology right?). Second, the government can attempt to remain silent on the question completely. But as we've just seen, when the government is comprehensively involved in culture, silence is impossible. The silence itself says loudly and clearly that religion is vaguely shameful. In reality, then, this second choice is just a variant of the first. The third option is an authentic pluralism that allows all faiths into the public square—where the government's own cultural efforts reflect those of the people and communities it serves. This third option is not only the most practical choice; it follows from who we are. It has, as the saying goes, the added advantage of being true.

It's not enough, though, simply to change the way the government looks at its citizens' culture. Its actions, which are governed by law, must change as well. So, in the next chapter, we'll look at how the law should change. When we last left the First Amendment, it was young and behaving badly—it was implicitly sanctioning state persecutions of religious minorities. Now it's long since grown up (you'll hardly recognize it). And like most of us at middle age, it has different problems.

THIRTEEN

The First Amendment at Midlife

Reflections on the incorporation doctrine—and
how two wrongs make a right of uncertain scope

In 1944, Rabbi Yoel Teitelbaum escaped the Holocaust. The leader of a community of Hasidic Jews known as the Satmars, Rabbi Teitelbaum had been ordered deported from Hungary to the Bergen-Belsen concentration camp. Nearly a million Hungarian Jews perished in the Holocaust; Rabbi Teitelbaum was one of the few to survive. Under the terms of a hideous bargain between Nazi official Adolf Eichmann and Rudolf Kastner of the Jewish Agency of Palestine, 1,600 Jews were allowed to escape, and Rabbi Teitelbaum was among them.

He used his freedom well. Following his escape, the Rabbi made his way to Brooklyn, where he founded a vibrant *kehillah*, or community, of Satmars. It was a bold attempt to preserve the Satmar way of life by transplanting it somewhere safe, somewhere beyond the reach of the Nazis.

They didn't even think about assimilating. Quite the contrary, the Satmars resolutely continued their traditions, and have ever since. In addition to their rigorous religious observance, they speak Yiddish; they refuse to watch television, listen to the radio, or read English-language publications; and they dress very distinctively. Yet, like so many other hardworking, determined bands of religious separatists, Rabbi Teitelbaum's Satmars found America fertile ground for their growing *kehillah*. It thrived. So much so that in 1977, the Satmars purchased an undeveloped subdivision in Monroe, New York, and legally incorporated it as a separate village, called Kiryas Joel. There they built a community, provided for a *shtibel,* or house of prayer, and established schools for their children. The Satmars hadn't assimilated, but they had, in a sense, integrated. They were no longer just a small subculture bobbing and weaving its way through civil society. Now they were their own village, a legal entity, with all the privileges and responsibilities this entailed.

Or so they thought. What happened next illustrates well what we might call the midlife crisis of the First Amendment.

How Do You Say Catch-22 in Yiddish?

Kiryas Joel, like any other small town, had its share of special-needs children. And like most small towns, it had limited resources for helping them. But, just like everyone else, the Satmars were entitled to government help. So the nearby Monroe public schools would send teachers to the Satmars' school in order to provide special education services for their handicapped children. So far, so good.

Then, in 1984, the Supreme Court held in *Aguilar v. Felton* that states could no longer send public school teachers to teach remedial classes at religious schools. This, the Court said, would violate the establishment clause. The Court worried that an overly intrusive surveillance system would be needed to keep an eye on the tutors. Otherwise, you see, the professional public school teachers would likely be so impressed by their temporary parochial school environs that they would begin to inject religion into their remedial math and English classes. (Yes, I'm serious. More in a moment.)

The *Aguilar* precedent doomed the Satmar schools' supplemental program. After *Aguilar,* handicapped children in the Satmar community had to travel to the Monroe public schools to get the government help to which they were entitled. It's easy to guess what happened next. In public school, the disabled children—some of whom were deaf or mentally retarded—were mocked mercilessly for their strange dress, accents and customs. All but one were pulled from the public schools. Those whose parents could afford it got private help, while the rest didn't get any help at all.

So the New York state legislature did what legislatures are supposed to do: it passed a law to meet the practical needs of its people. It created a new public school district for the village of Kiryas Joel so the children there could receive the special services that they needed in a public school hospitable to them.

But the Supreme Court struck this down as well, also under the First Amendment. This time it had a different anxiety: Since this was the first such accommodation the legislature had passed, how could the Court be certain that other, hypothetical groups would be treated equally in the future? (Why not just wait and see? If you're never allowed to pass the *first* one, how could there ever be more anyway? The Court didn't say.)

So the New York legislature passed a new law giving all municipalities in the state the right to form special school districts as long as they met certain criteria. But New York's highest court struck this down, too. The court said it didn't matter that other municipalities might someday meet these criteria; only Kiryas Joel currently did and that wasn't good enough under the establishment clause.

The Satmars, it seemed, just couldn't win: the New York legislature tried three times to accommodate their unique situation. Each time, the courts struck down the laws under the First Amendment's establishment clause. The courts finally accepted the fourth attempt—a law giving a broad swath of municipalities the right to apply for a special school district. In essence, the various courts all teamed up to rule that Kiryas Joel had to be the same as other villages if it wanted state help for its kids. It had no right to the help if it insisted on being different. Rather, the establishment clause required it to assimilate if it wanted government assistance.

Now, the establishment clause says, "*Congress* shall make no law respecting an establishment of religion." The New York state legislature obviously isn't "Congress." Moreover, as we've seen, the establishment clause was a compromise designed precisely to preserve the ability of states to legislate on matters like this. In the eighteenth and nineteenth centuries, no one would have looked twice at a state law focused (for good or ill) on a particular religious group. So what gives? Has the First Amendment somehow been amended?

Well, yes and no. What gives is that another constitutional amendment, enacted in the wake of the Civil War, was reinterpreted by the modern Supreme Court. And this reinterpreted amendment profoundly expanded, without quite amending, much of the Bill of Rights. It's an interesting story: two wrongs make a Right—and a big problem.

Establishment Clause, Inc.

Concerned that the southern states would not grant ex-slaves full legal equality with whites, the post–Civil War Congress had proposed, and the states had ratified, the Fourteenth Amendment, which reads in part:

> No State shall…abridge the privileges or immunities of citizens of the United States; nor shall any State deprive any person of life, liberty, or property, without due process of law.

Note the difference between the Bill of Rights originally and the Fourteenth Amendment. Originally, the Bill of Rights, as we've seen, applied only to the federal government, not to the states. For better or worse, the states could do as they pleased with regard to religion, speech, assembly and so forth, and the Bill of Rights offered no protection. The Fourteenth Amendment, by contrast, recognized a *federal* right to be free from *state* action.

But note also that the Fourteenth Amendment says nothing about religion, much less public school teachers tutoring needy religious school kids. So what does it have to do with things like the Kiryas Joel school district?

In 1925—several decades after it had become law—the Supreme Court began to hold that the Fourteenth Amendment "incorporated" some parts of the Bill of Rights, including the First Amendment. When the Fourteenth Amendment refers to "liberty," one of the things it means, the Court said, is the various sorts of freedom protected by the First Amendment. So "liberty" in the Fourteenth Amendment means, among other things, having the right against the state governments to freedom of speech and of the press, of assembly, of the free exercise of religion—and not to have the establishment clause violated, whatever that might mean.

Now, whether the Fourteenth Amendment was really designed to do this is still debated among academics. Nobody is exactly sure what the proponents of the Fourteenth Amendment had in mind. On the one hand, there is evidence that when they referred to the "privileges or immunities" of citizens of the United States, they had in mind at least some parts of the First Amendment. Many of the abolitionists had been clergymen who had been persecuted for their preaching against slavery. As early as 1819, the Reverend Jacob Gruber, a Methodist minister, had preached a sermon in Maryland condemning slavery, and was promptly arrested for inciting the slaves to revolt. North Carolina, in turn, had sentenced the Reverend Jesse McBride to twenty lashes, an hour in a pillory, and a year in prison for preaching an antislavery sermon. When the Fourteenth Amendment came up for ratification, its proponents seized on these sorts of stories and argued that the proposed amendment would protect religious freedom. One of the amendment's drafters, John Bingham, explained that one of the "privileges or immunities" of citizens of the United States was the right to "utter, according to conscience." So there is good reason to think that the privileges or immunities clause was meant to incorporate at least the free exercise clause. On the other hand, there is much less evidence that the proponents of the Fourteenth Amendment meant to incorporate the establishment clause, or anything else for that matter, into the word "liberty" in the due process clause.

The argument would now be almost entirely academic, except for one thing. While it is thoroughly settled as a legal matter that the establishment clause applies to the states, it's not at all settled what it means. And the "incorporation doctrine" is worth our consideration because of the great confusion that it has caused on that score.

But It Says...

It turns out that some provisions are more easily "incorporated" than others. To apply, say, the free speech clause or the free exercise clause against the states requires no great intellectual gymnastics; you just mentally substitute the word "states" for "Congress." But "incorporating" the First Amendment's establishment clause into the Fourteenth Amendment is not so simple. As we have seen, the purpose of the establishment clause was to make sure that the federal government would neither establish its own religion, nor interfere with the religions established in the states. Madison's hoped-for amendment providing that "no religion shall be established by law" was explicitly rejected because many rightly feared that it would authorize the federal government to *dis*establish state churches. That is why the framers selected the word "respecting" when describing what Congress could not do. Congress could not make any law "respecting" an establishment of religion because the drafters of the First Amendment wanted it to have the ability neither to establish any federal religion nor to *dis*establish any state religion.

Now, what does it mean to apply this "against" the states? That the states can't establish an official religion? Well then, what about the rest of the establishment clause—the part that was meant to allow state establishments to continue? How do you apply that "against" the states?

Put differently, how do you take a provision like the establishment clause—one designed only to pick which government, state or federal, gets to make a certain decision—and change it into an individual right without ever amending its language? How do you know where that right begins and ends? It's no longer defined by the words of the establishment clause itself— "Congress" can't mean Congress anymore; and "respecting" can't mean what it was intended to mean, either. Nor is it defined by the wording of the Fourteenth Amendment, into which it has been incorporated. "Liberty" is a very open-ended word. To say something is a "liberty," and nothing more, is not to say much. How, when or why is it legally protected, and how do you know when it's not? The incorporated establishment clause is a conundrum.

Let's be clear: it is just as immoral for a state government to repress religious liberty as it is for the federal government to repress it. Madison warned against this and he was right. The century and a half when the states were legally free to persecute were most emphatically not the good old days. As we've seen, they were the era of all sorts of injustices against Jews, Catholics and others. No, there is nothing about the era of state regulation of religion that should make anyone nostalgic. Congress's rejection of Madison's amendment was a big mistake.

But announcing that you've "incorporated" the First Amendment into a single word, "liberty," in another amendment is the wrong way to go about atoning for that mistake. And for our purposes it doesn't matter at all whether Congress and the states really did mean to incorporate the establishment clause, or the Supreme Court shoehorned it in as an exercise of sheer will. Whoever did it, the deed is now done, the law is settled and the problem it creates is the same: Incorporating the establishment clause creates a federal constitutional right—and at the same time leaves the scope of that right undefined by what the Constitution actually says.

Will the Real Establishment Clause Please Stand Up?

So, how do you construe a legal provision when the only thing you know for sure about it is that it no longer means what it says? Answer: You look elsewhere for substantive content that you can then read into it. History, philosophy, the framers' other writings, even their private correspondence have all been ransacked in the search for some substantive meaning to pour into the incorporated establishment clause. The result has been a free-for-all as Pilgrims, armed with their favorite snippets of history, etc., have squared off with Park Rangers, armed with theirs. Washington's Farewell Address duels with Jefferson's Letter to the Danbury Baptist Association, Madison's "Detached Memorandum" with the actions of the First Congress, radical secularism with near-theocracy.

The Supreme Court has been as fractured on the question as anyone, with some justices (Douglas, Black, Ginsburg,

Stevens, to name a few) being stridently, philosophically secularist. Stevens, for example, has never voted on the pro-religion side of any case that wasn't otherwise unanimous. Other justices (White, Rehnquist, Scalia and Thomas, for example) have read history as allowing the government to favor religion generally while being impartial among faiths. The two sides couldn't be more at odds—not only about what the incorporated establishment clause means but also over where to look to find out. When you add in a third, more pragmatic faction (Powell, O'Connor, et al.) that has sometimes sided with one faction and sometimes the other, the results have been unpredictable, to say the least.

At various times over the last few decades the establishment clause has meant some very odd things. It has meant, for example, that the state could *not* provide remedial math and science teachers in religious schools, but it *could* provide sign-language interpreters for math, science and all other classes—even for daily Mass. (Apparently interpreters, unlike the math teachers they interpret, will not be overwhelmed by the religious atmosphere.) The state violated the establishment clause when it provided busing from religious schools for field trips, but not when it provided busing to and from the religious school itself. At one point, it was legal for states to provide religious schools with film strips, but not the film projectors to show them, and it could lend them books, but not maps. (This led Senator Daniel Patrick Moynihan to quip that a future case would have to be about atlases, which are books of maps.)

If you think this reasoning is not just mistaken but positively incoherent, you're not alone. In fact, one of the few things that most justices have agreed upon in the past several decades is that the Supreme Court's establishment clause analysis has been in total disarray. The criticism began just a few years into incorporation, when Justice Jackson lamented that "the wall which the Court was professing to erect between Church and State has become even more warped and twisted than I expected." It continues unabated throughout all factions of the current Court. Arch-secularist Justice Stevens has derided the "Sisyphean task of trying to patch together the 'blurred, indistinct, and variable barrier'" that the Court had managed to create. He isn't the only one complaining. The swing votes have been just as blunt. Justice O'Connor has warned that the Court's establishment clause jurisprudence was confusing to the lower courts, which in turn were "making it more and more amorphous and distorted." And Justice Kennedy has criticized the Court's approach as "flawed in its fundamentals and unworkable in practice." Conservative Justice Scalia writes that "we are now so bold that we no longer feel the need even to pretend that our haphazard course of establishment clause decisions is governed by any principle."

This last statement was in reference to the Court's decision in *Kiryas Joel*, which is a perfect example of the disarray. The Court splintered so thoroughly in this case that its official summary of who joined what opinion is dizzying:

> Souter, J., announced the judgment of the Court and delivered the opinion of the Court with respect to Parts I, II-B, II-C, and III, in which Blackmun, Stevens, O'Connor, and Ginsburg, JJ., joined, and an opinion with respect to Parts II (introduction) and II-A, in which Blackmun, Stevens, and Ginsburg, JJ., joined. Blackmun, J., filed a concurring opinion. Stevens, J., filed a concurring opinion, in which Blackmun and Ginsburg, JJ., joined. O'Connor, J., filed an opinion concurring in part and concurring in the judgment. Kennedy, J., filed an opinion concurring in the judgment. Scalia, J., filed a dissenting opinion, in which Rehnquist, C. J., and Thomas, J., joined.

In essence, six of the nine justices thought the Kiryas Joel School District violated the First Amendment but couldn't entirely agree among themselves as to why. Four of the six wrote separately, peddling wildly different theories, while the three dissenters thought they were all completely wrong. Meanwhile, in another case, *Agostini v. Felton,* the Supreme Court voted 5-4 to overrule the *Aguilar* decision which had caused all the mischief in Kiryas Joel to begin with. But the opinion in that case too opened at least as many questions as it closed.

In short, the incorporated establishment clause has completely eluded principled interpretation.

So has the free exercise clause, though for different reasons.

Free Exercise, Inc.

Like the establishment clause, the free exercise clause has also been incorporated and applied to the states. At first glance, the free exercise clause appears to be fairly easy to incorporate; after all, it was an individual right to start with. So, like speech and the press and a whole host of other incorporated rights, the Supreme Court could incorporate the free exercise clause without too much of a strain.

If it really wanted to. The big question has always been, how much does it want to? Just what sorts of exercise are guaranteed to be free? Does the clause protect conscientious objectors? Or does it just protect, Plymouth-fashion, the right to dissent privately? And if it only protects private dissent, what good is it? The free speech clause protects that much and more.

As we've seen, the early trend was ominous, as the nineteenth-century Supreme Court nearly read free exercise out of existence. Almost a century later, the Court tried again. In 1963, it heard the appeal of Adell Sherbert, a Seventh-Day Adventist who was fired for refusing to work on the Sabbath, then denied unemployment benefits because she had been fired. The Court found that the unemployment compensation laws unfairly penalized her for exercising her religion. The Supreme Court ignored its nineteenth-century precedent and created a new rule: when a general law burdened religious exercise, the government had to grant an exemption, unless it could show a compelling reason for not doing so. In other words, the government had to have a very good excuse for interfering with the rights of conscience. Somewhere, the early Quakers were smiling.

Not everyone, though, was happy with *Sherbert.* An increasingly diverse society means an increasingly diverse number of exemptions. So, in *Employment Division v. Smith,* the Supreme Court took yet another look at the issue. Tired of that messy pluralism stuff, the Court laid out a new rule that was just as simple as the old one, but nearly its opposite: now, neutral and generally applicable laws *could* burden religion. Period. Exemptions need be considered only when such a law burdens both free exercise and another right, such as free speech or freedom of the press, or when the state is making decisions on a case-by-case basis.

Congress v. Court

Employment Division v. Smith was itself controversial. Congress overwhelmingly passed a law, the Religious Freedom Restoration Act (RFRA), that tried in effect to reinstate the *Sherbert* test. It applied to all levels of government, and stated that the compelling-state-interest test must be used.

But RFRA too provoked a great deal of disagreement, everyone waiting to see what the Supreme Court would do with the law. The Court got its chance from a most unlikely source: Boerne, Texas. Boerne is a small, once-rural town fending off the urban sprawl of nearby San Antonio. Desperate to keep its quaint main street (and in accordance with the Texas tradition of slapping a historical marker on anything that will stand still long enough), Boerne declared parts of its town "historical districts" and required government approval for any modification of the buildings there.

Which wouldn't have been a problem if it weren't for St. Peter Catholic Church. St. Peter's is a growing congregation, blessed by the same sprawl that cursed Boerne. The archdiocese recognized that the church's seventy-year-old facilities were outgrown and outmoded. The church simply couldn't function in them. The archdiocese made plans to renovate, but the city denied it the necessary permits. The historical commission wasn't about to let the church remodel its "historical" building. The church claimed that the city was violating RFRA, and the city claimed that RFRA was unconstitutional. So the city fought the church, all the way to the Supreme Court, which wasted no time in striking down RFRA because, the Court said, Congress had overstepped its bounds. Free exercise shriveled once again.

But Congress itself wasted no time in wading back into the fray: it passed the Religious Land Use and Institutionalized Persons Act (RLUIPA) to protect the rights of St. Peter's and thousands of other places of worship. The situation in Boerne was not unusual: zoning of religious property is a hot-button issue across the country, with bitter disagreements fueled by the tax-free status of houses of worship. This has led some cities to exclude places of worship from large swaths of land and place onerous restrictions on others. The battle can be most difficult for minority religions, which have neither the private funds to litigate nor the public support to win variances. RLUIPA protects places of worship involved in these fights and allows them the freedom to build and expand. It also prevents cities from designating "church-free zones," and from treating places of worship more harshly than similar secular land uses. So free exercise is growing modestly in the land use area.

But as of this writing, an assortment of Park Rangers and bureaucrats are challenging the constitutionality of RLUIPA and there's no telling what the Supreme Court will do. Moreover, other sorts of conscientious objectors are at the mercy of the legislatures—and even then, an accommodation granted by the legislature is itself at the mercy of the Supreme Court's unstable interpretation of the establishment clause. The Court has upheld some legislative accommodations (like exceptions from civil rights laws, so churches aren't forced to hire ministers of another faith), but struck down others (remember Kiryas Joel?).

In short, the incorporated free exercise clause isn't the conundrum that the establishment clause is; it's just a little scary. When it was initially applied to the federal government, the free exercise clause limited only Congress. Now that it's been incorporated into the Fourteenth Amendment, it restricts the actions of "the state." While its substantive meaning wasn't changed by its incorporation, its scope was. What formerly applied only to the legislative branch of the federal government now applied to every official or employee of every state—from public school teachers to zoning commissioners, from police officers to dogcatchers. Meanwhile, the number of different faiths in America has exploded.

The vast extension in the scope of the free exercise clause has given the federal courts the constitutional equivalent of vertigo as they contemplate allowing the clause to mean what it says and yet apply it across the board in defense of all faiths against every bureaucrat high and low. This is, to a degree, understandable. Having virtually everyone constitutionally exempt from one requirement or another seems no way to run a railroad.

You Can't Get There from Here

So, what's the solution? Purists (Pilgrims, mostly) believe we should abandon incorporation and once again let the states do what they will with religion—or else amend the First Amendment to say whatever it is we want it to mean.

Neither one is ever going to happen. And on reflection, we don't really want it to. Dis-incorporation takes us right back to where we started—states winning the power struggle over religious freedom. It's a statement about who makes the rules, not a solution that will get us the right ones. Ask the Catholics in Philadelphia or the Jews in any state how well the old system worked. Another amendment isn't the solution, either. If Madison could get only half a loaf, imagine the compromises a modern legislature would be forced to make. The end result would probably look something like the court opinion in *Kiryas Joel*.

Pragmatists (Park Rangers, mostly) take the opposite view. They prefer to ignore the problem and muddle through. (And why not? The Park Rangers are mostly winning under the status quo.)

The most strident Park Rangers propose yet another solution. According to them, the words of the incorporated establishment clause should control its meaning—so long as you reinterpret those words to mean something different from what they originally did. For them, "respecting an establishment of religion" should now be reread to mean "mentioning any religion at all." The government must have nothing to do with religion and nothing to say about it. A convenient fit with the Park Rangers' basic project.

But those aren't workable solutions either. Dishonesty in constitutional interpretation breeds lawlessness. A law that means nothing, that is bent to the contours of each new situation or that can be reread at will, ceases to be law at all. This particular bit of dishonesty is also inhuman; as we've seen, it leaves our spiritual side out of public culture.

What to do? Admit that there are no such things as square circles and give up on the incorporated establishment clause altogether. This doesn't mean giving up on incorporation generally. And it certainly doesn't mean reverting to the days of state-law persecution. It means only that the incorporated establishment clause has demonstrated that it is uniquely dysfunctional. It is incapable of answering our questions, so we should stop asking it any.

The incorporated free exercise clause, on the other hand, is perfectly functional, if judicially repressed. If allowed to mean what it says, it could be quite potent. As incorporated, it could codify the full-throated natural right to religious liberty while making moot the conundrum of the incorporated establishment clause. That is, it could protect true free exercise—the freedom "to embrace, to profess and to observe," in Madison's words. And as Madison argued his entire life, the right to free exercise itself precludes establishment.

The free exercise clause, in short, could protect us from both the Pilgrims and the Park Rangers.

But is all this religious liberty stuff actually worth the trouble? Is it really that important? Sure, Roger Williams and James Madison thought so, but they're dead. Who's to say it's important now? Mohammed-from-Mecca, whom we'll meet in the next and final chapter.

FOURTEEN

The Right to Be Wrong

Ending the culture war

A call-in show? No problem, I thought. I had done plenty in the roughly ten years since I'd started the Becket Fund. I was used to fielding slightly off-point calls from Danny-in-Dubuque. And I thought I'd seen or heard it all. Then came the gig on the Arab satellite network Al-Jazeera. The first caller was definitely not Danny-in-Dubuque but, literally, Mohammed-from-Mecca. And his question was very much on-point. He addressed it to the moderator: "Why are you dialoguing with this infidel? Why not just wage jihad on him?"

Well, I thought from the safety of my satellite hook-up in Washington, a Pilgrim's Pilgrim. This should be interesting.

Evidently it was—at least enough to get me invited back for another round on Al-Jazeera, as well as for a six-hour series on one of its competitors, the London-based Al-Mustakillah. What did I have to say that was so interesting? The same thing I've laid out in the previous chapters here: That while we couldn't agree on who God is, we could and should agree on who we are. That we share a thirst for the true and the good, and a conscience that drives our quest to find them and then insists that we embrace and express publicly what we believe we've found. That if we can agree on this much, then we share a profound truth: The truth about man is that man is born to seek freely the truth about God.

Mohammed-from-Mecca would still be perfectly free to call me an infidel and I could still think he was confused. We could each believe the other was wrong. We could even warn each other of dreadful things in the hereafter as a consequence of being wrong. But in the here-and-now we would each recognize that the other had—in truth—the right to be wrong.

I wish I could report having won him over. It turned out he actually had hung up while the translator was still hemming and hawing over whether to let me in on the fact that their very first caller had suggested doing me in. But judging from the calls on my follow-up appearances, this was an idea that could translate into Islamic thought. (Which is, of course, the whole beauty of *universal* human rights in the first place.)

Why did they take me seriously? For that matter, what was I doing on Al-Jazeera, anyway? The reason I was welcome was that I had already put my money where my mouth was. I had successfully defended the right of two Newark Police officers, who were Sunni Muslims, to grow their beards. In other words, I was welcomed on Al-Jazeera (except by Mohammed-from-Mecca) for the same reason I still get invited to Hasidic Jewish weddings. I had demonstrated respect for their consciences by successfully defending their rights. This, in turn, had won me a respectful hearing as to just why they should dialogue with this infidel rather than peremptorily wage jihad on me.

Writ large, that is the solution to the culture war. Respect for others' consciences, even when we're sure they are wrong, is contagious. Not because it's nice. (In fact, the postmodern consensus seems to be that it's *not* nice to call anybody wrong.) Rather, it's contagious because it conveys an important idea: Whether it's a tradition as old and venerable as Buddhism or as new and flaky as parking-barrier worship doesn't matter. Because of how we're made, we are each free—within broad limits—to follow what we believe to be true in the manner that our consciences say we must. That is, we are free to celebrate our beliefs in public and try respectfully to persuade others of them. We are free, ultimately, to organize our entire lives around them.

So, of course, are those with whom we disagree. And we can grant this point with complete integrity. We can each recognize the other's freedom without surrendering our own allegiance to the truth. We're free to insist that others are wrong for the same reason they're free to insist that we are.

The truth is, we each have the right to be wrong.

Notes

Chapter 1: Of Pilgrims and Park Rangers

page

3–4 *Japanese Tea Garden*—The story of the sacred parking barrier was covered in a series of articles in the *San Francisco Chronicle*. See Phillip Matier and Andrew Ross, "New Age Shrine Moved from Park," *S.F. Chronicle*, January 21, 1994, p. A17.

5 *Columnist Andrew Sullivan*—Andrew Sullivan, "This Is a Religious War," *New York Times Magazine*, October 7, 2001, p. 44.

Chapter 2: Pluralism, Conscience and Community

9 *when they reached America*—For a thorough yet brief account of events referred to in this chapter and the next, see Richard D. Brown and Jack Tager, *Massachusetts: A Concise History* (University of Massachusetts Press, 2000).

10 *fled to Holland*—The Pilgrims settled first in Amsterdam. Then, when they separated from some of their fellow separatists over doctrinal issues, they moved to the city of Leyden, where they were left to pursue their idiosyncratic Christianity in peace. William Bradford, *Of Plymouth Plantation*, ed. Samuel Eliot Morison (Knopf, 1984) (1650), pp. 16–17.

10 *not up to Pilgrim standards*—Ibid., p. 25, note 8.

10 *pull up stakes and leave*—Ibid., pp. 23–25.

10 *look the other way*—Ibid., pp. 28–30.

11 *financial backers in London*—Ibid., pp. 44–45, see note 9.

11–12 *for the fledgling colony*—"In the name of God, Amen," it began. Having started their journey "for the Glory of God, and advancement of the Christian Faith," the little band of saints and strangers now "solemnly and mutually in the presence of God and one of another," bound themselves "together into a Civil Body Politic, for...furtherance" of those ends. Ibid., pp. 75–76.

12 *heritage of religious liberty*—See Arlin Adams and Charles Emmerich, *A Nation Dedicated to Religious Liberty* (University of Pennsylvania Press, 1990), p. 5, which takes the more traditional view of religious liberty in Plymouth.

12 *Among other things*—Lyford was in trouble on many counts. There is, however, no reason to believe his attempt to establish an Anglican congregation would have been any more welcome had he been a model citizen. Bradford, *Of Plymouth Plantation*, pp. 147–63.

12 *"apart on the Lord's Day"*—Ibid., p. 151.

13–14 *or of his worship*—Forward to the Revision of the New Plymouth Laws, 1658, available at http://personal.pitnet.net/primarysources/newplymouth-laws.html.

16 *ingenuity of fools*—The origin of this aphorism is unclear. Several sources attribute it to Gene Brown, but two other quite similar statements are attributed to humorist Douglas Adams.

17 *more mainstream religions*—*Church of Lukumi Babalu Aye v. City of Hialeah*, 508 U.S. 520, 541-42 (1993).

18 *with a consent decree*—*Haven Shores Community Church v. City of Grand Haven*, File No. 1:00-cv-175 (W.D. Mich.) (consent decree signed December 20, 2000).

Chapter 3: Religion in Public Culture

22 *anybody could fill it*—James Baker, *The Pilgrims as People: Understanding the Plymouth Colonists*, Plimoth Plantation website, Smithsonian Institution, *at* http://plimoth.org/learn/history/colonists/PilgrimPeople.asp.

22 *in addition to food*—A colonist described the festivities as follows: "Our harvest being gotten in, our governor sent four men on fowling, that so we might after a special manner rejoice together, after we had gathered the fruit of our labors. They four in one day killed as much fowl as, with a little help beside, served the Company almost a week. At which time, amongst other recreations, we exercised our arms, many of the Indians coming amongst us, and amongst the rest their greatest king, Massasoit with some 90 men, whom for three days we entertained and feasted.

And they went out and killed five deer which they brought to the plantation and bestowed on our Governor and upon the Captain and others." Edward Winslow's letter describing the feast, written December 11, 1621, reprinted in William Bradford, *Of Plymouth Plantation*, ed. Samuel Eliot Morison (Knopf, 1984) (1650), p. 90, note 8.

22 *called them out to work*—Ibid., p. 97.

22 *in Plymouth splitting lumber*—Meanwhile, the crew aboard the *Mayflower*, which was still in Plymouth Harbor at the time, celebrated with a Christmas ration of beer. Edward Winslow and William Bradford, *Mourt's Relation: A Journal of the Pilgrims at Plymouth, 1622*, Part 1, ed. Caleb Johnson (University of Virginia, 2003) (1622), available at Electronic Text Center, University of Virginia Library, http://etext.lib.virginia.edu/users/deetz/Plymouth/mourt1.html.

22 *veteran colonists away to work*—Bradford, *Of Plymouth Plantation*, p. 97.

23 *reveling in the streets*—Ibid., p. 97.

23 *outlawed Christmas for twenty-two years*—From 1659 until 1681. James P. Walsh, "Holy Time and Sacred Space in Puritan New England," *American Quarterly*, vol. 32 (1980), pp. 82–87.

25 *Metzl v. Leininger*—57 F.3d 618 (7th Cir. 1994).

26 *as good as any*—*Brindenbaugh v. O'Bannon*, 1999 WL 517169 (7th Cir. 1999).

26 *ACLU v. Sycamore Community School District*—A case challenging a school district's practice of closing on Yom Kippur was filed by the ACLU in the Southern District of Ohio in 1999. "ACLU Sues over Ohio School District's Policy on Religious Holidays," American Civil Liberties Union Homepage, *at* http://www.aclu.org/ReligiousLiberty/ReligiousLiberty.cfm?ID=8662&c=139 (August 25, 1999).

26 *Ganulin v. United States*—71 F. Supp. 2d 824 (S.D. Ohio 1999).

26 *Bonham v. District of Columbia Library Admin.*—989 F.2d 1242 (D.C. Cir. 1993).

26 *Brindenbaugh v. O'Bannon*—1999 WL 517169 (7th Cir. 1999).

26 *Granzier v. Middleton*—173 F.3d 568 (6th Cir. 1999); see

also *Koenick v. Felton,* 190 F.3d 259 (4th Cir. 1999); *Mandel v. Hodges,* 54 Cal. App. 3d 596 (Sup. Ct. Cal. 1976).

Chapter 4: What about Proselytizing?

30 *"City upon a Hill"*—John Winthrop, *A Model of Christian Charity* (1630), available at The Religious Freedom Page, University of Virginia, http://religiousfreedom.lib.virginia.edu/sacred/charity.html.

30 *"among whom we have lived"*—Ibid.

30 *"such a Covenant"*—Ibid.

30 *for some repeat offenders*—For a lengthy account of such punishments, including branding, in New England, see Alice Morse Earle, *Curious Punishments of Bygone Days* (Kessinger Publishing Co., 2003) (1929), available at http://www.getchwood.com/punishments/curious. According to Earle, Quakers in New England were branded with an H for heresy.

31 *belonged to the Indians*—John Winthrop, *Winthrop's Journal,* vol. 1, ed. James Kendall Hosmer (Barnes & Noble, Inc., 1966) (1790), pp. 116–17.

31 *wasn't Christian at all*—Ibid.

31 *was actually anti-Christian*—Ibid., p. 142. Some of Williams' positions were truly idiosyncratic. For example, Williams opposed the colony's loyalty oath—not because he was against either loyalty or oaths, but because requiring an oath of everyone would inevitably cause some to take the Lord's name in vain and would also cause godly magistrates to be in communion with the ungodly when they administered the oath to them. Ibid., p. 149.

32 *all nations and countries*—Roger Williams, *The Bloudy Tenet, Of Persecution for Cause of Conscience* (1644), available at Philip B. Kurland and Ralph Lerner, *The Founders' Constitution* (University of Chicago Press, 1986), http://press-pubs.uchicago.edu/founders/documents/amendI_religions4.html. This comes very close to saying that it is a God-given universal human right to be able to practice and preach all manner of religions. The language of "permission" being "granted" is the language of tolerance, not of rights. (More in Chapter 5.) But since Williams' basic idea is more than a century ahead of its time, maybe we shouldn't be picky about his terminology.

32 *"breach of the Sabbath"*—*Winthrop's Journal,* vol. 1, p. 62.

32 *"could not intermeddle"*—Ibid., p. 154.

34 *banished in October 1635*—Ibid., pp. 162–63.

34 *"others to his opinions"*—Ibid., p. 168.

34 *later become Rhode Island*—Ibid.

34 *They persecuted it*—Ibid., p. 262; *Winthrop's Journal,* vol. 2, p. 81.

35 *"nimble wit and active spirit"*—John Winthrop, *A Short Story of the Rise, Reign, and Ruin of the Antinomians,* ed. David D. Hall (Duke University Press, 1990) (1644), p. 213. The record of Hutchinson's trial survives in two versions, a short version written by Winthrop, and a longer anonymous version. The original of the longer version has been lost, but it was reprinted a century later in a history of the colony written by her great-great-grandson, Thomas Hutchinson. Both versions are reprinted in Hall. The following is from the Winthrop version, except where noted.

35 *"and weak parts"*—*Winthrop's Journal,* vol. 1, p. 299.

36 *a growing circle of men*—See ibid., p. 195, note 1; see also Winthrop, *Short Story,* p. 217.

36 *"Protestants and papists"*—Paul Johnson, "God and the Americans," *Commentary,* vol. 99, no. 1 (January 1995).

36 *dishonoring the authorities*—Massachusetts General Laws, Heresie (1646), reprinted in Donald S. Lutz, ed., *Colonial Origins of the American Constitution: A Documentary History* (Liberty Fund, 1998), available at http://oll. libertyfund.org/Texts/LFBooks/Lutz0397/ColonialOrigins/ 0013_Bk.html.

36 *welfare of the community*—Winthrop, *Short Story,* p. 347.

36–37 *who were agitating the colony*—Ibid., p. 216.

37 *"but for your practice"*—Ibid.

37 *brought to ruin*—Ibid., pp. 272–73.

37 *"rule in all things"*—Ibid., p. 274.

37 *best to silence her*—Winthrop also alludes to the lesson learned from Munster, Germany, where in 1534, Anabaptists who had taken over the city were massacred by a rival Protestant faction. Ibid., p. 275. It's a typical seventeenth-century assumption: religious differences can be settled only by force of arms. Indeed, when the dissidents were sentenced, they were required to surrender the muskets upon which all wilderness families depended. Ibid., p. 279.

38 *with the Supreme Court—Board of Airport Commissioners v. Jews for Jesus,* 482 U.S. 569 (1987).

38 *Jehovah's Witnesses—Cantwell v. Connecticut,* 310 U.S. 296 (1940).

38 *Hare Krishnas—International Society for Krishna Consciousness v. Lee,* 505 U.S. 672 (1992).

38 *the Unification Church—Larson v. Valente,* 456 U.S. 228 (1982).

38 *striking down the order—Rigdon v. Perry,* 962 F. Supp. 150 (D.D.C. 1997).

38 *So has sex—Cf.* John T. Noonan Jr., *The Lustre of Our Country: The American Experience of Religious Freedom* (University of California Press, 1998), p. 2.

40 *flogging for any who persisted*—Ibid., p. 51.

40 *"with a hot iron"*—See Meredith Baldwin Weddle, *Walking in the Way of Peace: Quaker Pacifism in the Seventeenth Century* (Oxford University Press, 2000), p. 85. Weddle's book gives an excellent, detailed history of Quaker sufferings in New England. The text of the statute is available at: http://depts.clackamas.cc.or.us/banyan/1.1/moss3.htm.

40 *lost his right ear*—Weddle, *Walking in the Way of Peace,* p. 90.

40 *"upon pain of death"*—Statute reprinted in William Sewell, *The History of the Rise, Increase, and Progress, of the Christian People Called Quakers* (Uriah Hunt, 1832), vol. 1, pp. 222–23, available at The Quaker Writings Homepage, http://www.qhpress.org/quakerpages/qwhp/masslaw.htm.

40 *"and gain Proselites"*—Massachusetts General Laws, Quakers (1656).

40 *"infected" with them*—Sewell, *The History of the Rise, Increase, and Progress.*

41 *"comely young woman"*—Winthrop, *Short Story,* p. 280.

41 *preaching in Massachusetts*—Rufus Jones, *Quakers in the American Colonies* (W. W. Norton, 1966), p. 89.

41 *executed just days before*—Margaret Hope Bacon, *The Quiet Rebels: The Story of the Quakers in America* (Basic Books, 1969), pp. 32–33.

42 *borders of the Bay Colony itself*—Noonan, *The Lustre of Our Country,* p. 52.

42 *"intrusions of the Quakers"*—Ibid., p. 53.

Chapter 5: Heavens No, We Won't Go

46 *directly in jail*—Margaret Hope Bacon, *The Quiet Rebels: The Story of the Quakers in America* (Basic Books, 1969), p. 39.

47 *imprisoned alongside him*—Jay Worrall, *The Friendly Virginians: America's First Quakers* (Iberian Publishing, 1994), pp. 32–34.

47 *considered an enemy*—Ibid., p. 202.

47 *anyone who refused the oath*—Ibid.

47 *came close to starvation*—Bacon, *The Quiet Rebels*, pp. 73–74.

47 *allowing the Quakers to return*—Ibid., p. 73.

47–48 *in his militia unit*—Peter Brock, *Liberty and Conscience: A Documentary History of the Experiences of Conscientious Objectors in America through the Civil War* (Oxford University Press, 2002), pp. 22–24.

48 *"interest of the nation may justify"*—Bacon, *The Quiet Rebels*, pp. 75–76.

48 *by swearing* or by affirming—Art. II, § 1.

49 *"split [his] brains"*—Brock, *Liberty and Conscience*, pp. 7–8.

49 *man's meager profits*—Ibid., p. 8.

49 *one hundred pounds of tobacco*—Lillian Schlissel, ed., *Conscience in America: A Documentary History of Conscientious Objection in America, 1757–1967* (E. P. Dutton, 1968), p. 29.

49 *anyone who opposed military service*—Meredith Baldwin Weddle, *Walking in the Way of Peace: Quaker Pacifism in the Seventeenth Century* (Oxford University Press, 2000), p. 93.

49 *"goods and cattle"*—Brock, *Liberty and Conscience*, p. 10.

50 *fines for refusal to serve*—Weddle, *Walking in the Way of Peace*, pp. 165, 200.

50 *strictly voluntary militia*—Stephen M. Kohn, *Jailed for Peace: The History of American Draft Law Violators, 1658–1985* (Greenwood Press, 1986), p. 9.

50 *between 18 and 53*—Revolutionary War Military Abstract Card File, Pennsylvania State Archives, http://www.digitalarchives.state.pa.us/archive.asp.

50 *pay soldiers or buy weapons*—Some Quakers also opposed the fines for deeper, more rankling reasons. They wanted to

know what they were being fined *for.* They believed freedom of conscience was something they possessed inherently,
not something the law created. How did the legislature get
away with taxing them for something it had no lawful control over? Brock, *Liberty and Conscience,* pp. 84–87.

50 *seizures were supposed to cover*—Kohn, *Jailed for Peace,*
p. 6; Brock, *Liberty and Conscience,* pp. 8–9, 83–84.

51 *new state constitutions*—Kohn, *Jailed for Peace,* p. 10.
Rhode Island, which asked Congress for a federal constitutional amendment, is not included in this list because it did
not write a new constitution during this time period.

51 *"render military service in person"*—James Madison, Pro-
posals to the Congress for a Bill of Rights, reprinted in
Schlissel, *Conscience in America,* p. 47.

51 *protecting religious conscientious objection*—The states
were North Carolina, Virginia, Rhode Island and Pennsylvania. Kohn, *Jailed for Peace,* p. 14, note 32.

51 *tied up and beaten*—Kohn, *Jailed for Peace,* pp. 20–21.
This quotes an account printed in the *Liberator* on August
21, 1863.

51 *dropped their weapons*—Edward Needles Wright, *Conscientious Objectors in the Civil War* (University of
Pennsylvania Press, 1931), pp. 176–77.

51 *petitioning President Lincoln*—Brock, *Liberty and Conscience,* p. 114.

51 *former slaves as well*—Schlissel, *Conscience in America,* p.
98.

52 *"orthodox belief in God"*—U.S. v. Seeger, 380 U.S. 163,
166 (1965).

53 *Medal of Honor*—Desmond Doss, a Seventh-Day Adventist, won the Medal of Honor for his service as a medic in
Okinawa during WWII. Thomas W. Bennett was awarded
the Medal posthumously for his service as a medic in Vietnam.

55 *"essential interest of the nation"*—Bacon, *The Quiet
Rebels,* pp. 75–76.

Chapter 6: Why Tolerance Is Intolerable

58 *she, too, was a Catholic*—John T. Noonan Jr., *The Lustre
of Our Country: The American Experience of Religious*

Freedom (University of California Press, 1998), p. 365.

58 *religiously tumultuous England*—Ibid., p. 49.

58 *the Blessed Virgin Mary and Henrietta Maria*—Ibid., p. 365.

58 *Judgments and Consciences*—James H. Hutson, *Religion and the Founding of the American Republic* (Library of Congress, 1998), pp. 12–13 (emphasis added).

59 *back to England in chains*—Ibid., p. 15.

59 *American legal lexicon*—Ibid.

59 *"matter of religion"*—Maryland Toleration Act of 1649, available at The Avalon Project, Yale Law School, http://www.yale.edu/lawweb/avalon/amerdoc/maryland_toleration.htm.

59 *certain forms of heresy*—In particular, the Act prescribed death for anti-Trinitarians. Hutson, *Religion and the Founding*, p. 15.

59 *repealed the Act of Toleration*—Aubrey C. Land, *Colonial Maryland: A History* (Kraus International Publications, 1981), p. 51.

59 *executing four of them*—Hutson, *Religion and the Founding*, p. 15.

59 *so-called Act of Toleration*—Ibid.; Land, *Colonial Maryland*, p. 92.

60 *from worshipping publicly*—Thomas Peterman, *Catholics in Colonial Delmarva* (Cooke Publishing Co., 1996), pp. 161–67.

60 *"Perswasion or Practice"*—Hutson, *Religion and the Founding*, p. 11.

60 *had already moved there*—Ibid.

61 *Dunkards, Schwenkfelders and Moravians*—Ibid., pp. 11–12.

61 *usher in the millennium*—Ibid., p. 12.

61 *Pennsylvania's new constitution in 1776*—Patricia Bonomi, *Under the Cope of Heaven: Religion, Society and Politics in Colonial America* (Oxford University Press, 1995), p. 36.

61 *deserted the assembly altogether*—Peter Brock, *Liberty and Conscience: A Documentary History of the Experiences of Conscientious Objectors in America through the Civil War* (Oxford University Press, 2002), pp. 5–6. The dual pres-

sures of war and threats from the Crown led Quakers to desert the legislature.

61 *oath of allegiance to the king*—The story of Pennsylvania's oath requirements and the text of the oath are available at the Pennsylvania State Archives website: Oaths of Fidelity and Abjuration, Pennsylvania State Archives, http://www.docheritage.state.pa.us/documents/oathsfidelity. asp.

61 *"acknowledges the being of a God"*—1776 Constitution, Declaration of Rights, Art. II, available at Pennsylvania State Archives, http://www.docheritage.state.pa.us/documents/constitutiontrans.asp.

61 *excluding all but Christians*—1776 Constitution, Frame of Government, Section X, available at Pennsylvania State Archives, http://www.docheritage.state.pa.us/documents/constitutiontrans.asp.

62 *the term 'government' itself*—He was influenced by the comprehension movement, a cause that sought to gain religious freedom by turning the Church of England into a kind of catch-all so broad that all Christian sects would be included. Yet he opposed a Bill of Comprehension proposed in England. Why? The usual reason. Comprehension wasn't broad enough to comprehend Quakers. Mary Maples Dunn, *William Penn, Politics and Conscience* (Princeton University Press, 1967), pp. 69–70.

62 *belonged only to Him*—Ibid., p. 51.

62 *"never could be in the right"*—William Penn, *Account of My Life Since Convincement*, reprinted in Richard Dunn & Mary Maples Dunn, ed., *The Papers of William Penn*, vol. 3 (University of Pennsylvania Press, 1986), p. 337.

63 *"full livertie in religious concernements"*—Charter of Rhode Island and Providence Plantations, available at The Avalon Project, Yale Law School, http://www.yale.edu/lawweb/avalon/states/ri04.htm (1663).

64 *"stinks in God's nostrils"*—Roger Williams, *The Bloudy Tenet, Of Persecution for Cause of Conscience* (1644), available at Philip B. Kurland and Ralph Lerner, *The Founders' Constitution* (University of Chicago Press, 1986), http://press-pubs.uchicago.edu/founders/documents/amendI_religions4.html.

64 *"all nations and countries"*—Ibid.

65 *"duly and faithfully observed"*—Fundamental Constitutions of Carolina, Art. 97. He added that "Jews, heathens, and other dissenters from the purity of Christian religion may not be scared and kept at a distance from it, but, by having an opportunity of acquainting themselves with the truth and reasonableness of its doctrines...be won over to embrace and unfeignedly receive the truth." Available at The Avalon Project, Yale Law School, http://www.yale.edu/lawweb/avalon/states/nc05.htm.

65 *registered it with the government*—Ibid.

65 *receive public funds*—Fundamental Constitutions of Carolina, Art. 96. See also note on Art. 96, available at The Avalon Project.

65 *all-Anglican Assembly*—John Wesley Brinsfield, *Religion and Politics in Colonial South Carolina* (Southern Historical Press, 1983), p. 23.

65 *could perform marriages*—Ibid., p. 24.

65 *"almost to a mania"*—Ibid., p. 47.

65 *incorporating churches and voting*—Ibid.

65 *"all denominations of Christian protestants"*—Ibid., p. 123.

66 *allowed to legally incorporate*—Ibid., pp. 123–24.

66 *in Charleston until 1790*—Ibid., p. 47.

66 *hold office there until 1868*—Jonathan D. Sarna, *Religion and State in the American Jewish Experience* (University of Notre Dame Press, 2000), p. 83.

66 *atheists and Catholics*—John Locke, *A Letter Concerning Toleration,* reprinted in John Horton and Susan Mendes, *John Locke: A Letter Concerning Toleration in Focus* (Routledge, 1991) (1689), p. 51.

66 *any non-Catholic nation*—Ibid. at pp. 46–47.

67 *could even vote*—"The Early Years," United Church of Christ, available at http://1stcong.weblogger.com/stories/storyReader$1178. This history relies heavily on *Saints and Strangers,* George Willison's popular and influential work chronicling the history of Plymouth.

Chapter 7: From Tolerance to Natural Rights

71 *dissenting Protestants had weathered*—Under English law,
the canons of the Church of England could not be insulted,
Protestant ministers outside the Church of England could
not preach unless they swore to uphold Christian doctrines
enumerated by statute, and Catholic priests who celebrated
Mass could be punished by penalties as severe as life
imprisonment. John T. Noonan Jr., *The Lustre of Our
Country: The American Experience of Religious Freedom*
(University of California Press, 1998), p. 57. Persecution of
Protestant dissenters—i.e., Protestants who remained outside the Church of England—in particular had waned
considerably since the Acts of Toleration in 1688 and 1711.
Local communities, however, often did not take kindly to
the more obstreperous kind of dissenter, and took full
advantage of what powers remained to punish them.

71 *preaching without a license*—Ibid., p. 67.

71 *could not in conscience do*—Ibid.

71 *beyond its pale*—Ibid., p. 68.

71 *off to be flogged*—Ibid., p. 67.

71–72 *"pray for Liberty of Conscience"*—Ibid., p. 68.

72 *"Dictates of Conscience..."*—Ibid., p. 69.

72 *"dictates of Conscience"*—Ralph Louis Ketcham, *James
Madison: A Biography* (University Press of Virginia, 1990),
p. 72. George Mason's version had said that "Religion, or
the Duty we owe to our...Creator...can be governed only be
Reason and Conviction, not by *Force* or Violence"; Madison replaced "Force" with the broader and more
ambiguous "Compulsion," suggesting that subtler forms of
coercion as well as physical force could also violate one's
rights. Noonan, *The Lustre of Our Country*, p. 69.

72 *"peculiar emoluments or privileges"*—Ibid.

72–73 *"Charity towards Each other"*—James Madison, *The
Papers of James Madison*, vol. 1. ed. William T. Hutchinson (University of Chicago Press, 1963), pp. 172–75.

73 *in its privileged position*—Noonan, *The Lustre of Our
Country*, p. 70.

73 *on account of religion*—Ibid.

74 *many of its supporting laws*—While many statutes explicitly regulating religious opinions were in fact repealed,
others remained in place, including the requirement
restricting public office to those acknowledging the exis-

tence of God, of the Trinity, and affirming the authority of Scripture. Ibid., p. 71.

74 *burn at the stake*—Ibid.

76 *Virginia House of Delegates*—Thomas Jefferson, *The Life and Selected Writings of Thomas Jefferson*, ed. Adrienne Koch and William Peden (Modern Library, 1993), p. xii.

76–77 *"infringement of natural right"*—A Bill for Establishing Religious Freedom, reprinted in *Thomas Jefferson: Writings*, ed. Merrill D. Peterson (Library of America, 1984), pp. 347–48.

77 *any worship or ministry*—Ibid., pp. 346–47.

77 *increasingly rickety establishment*—Thomas Jefferson, *Autobiography*, reprinted in *The Life and Selected Writings of Thomas Jefferson*, ed. Koch and Peden, pp. 41–42.

77 *"teachers of the Gospel"*—Noonan, *The Lustre of Our Country*, p. 71.

78 *"cunning of the old fox"*—Ibid., p. 72.

78 *"as these may dictate"*—James Madison, Memorial and Remonstrance Against Religious Assessments (1785), available at Religious Freedom Page, University of Virginia, http://religiousfreedom.lib.virginia.edu/sacred/madison_m&r_1785.html. Emphasis added.

79 *"of divine origin"*—Ibid.

79 *"which has convinced us"*—Ibid.

79 *"an unalienable right"*—Ibid.

79 *"to the Universal Sovereign"*—Ibid.

79–80 *"exempt from its cognizance"*—Ibid.

80 *Henry's plan was "crushed."*—Noonan, *The Lustre of Our Country*, p. 74.

80 *mothballed in 1779*—Ibid., pp. 74–75.

Chapter 8: Inalienable Rights, Slightly Alienated

83 *Benjamin Franklin and John Adams*—Franklin, Adams, Livingston and Sherman were all on the committee assigned to draft the declaration, but Jefferson did the bulk of the writing, with drafts submitted to Adams, Franklin and Sherman, of whom Adams and Franklin suggested changes. "Declaring Independence: Drafting the Documents," Library of Congress Exhibitions, at http://www.loc.gov/exhibits/declara/declara3.html. The rough draft is available at

http://www.loc.gov/exhibits/declara/ruffdrft.html.

83 *even more—about 200*—Paul Finkelman, *Slavery and the Founders: Race and Liberty in the Age of Jefferson* (M. E. Sharpe, 2001), p. 242, note 4.

83 *he had freed only 3*—Ibid. at p. 153. All eight slaves freed by Jefferson (three during his life and five in his will) were members of the Hemings family. Ibid., p. 154.

83 *selling at least 85*—Ibid., p. 130.

83 *pay his debts*—Ibid.

83 *created equal to him*—Ibid., p. 239, note 100.

84 *"emancipation of human nature"*—Thomas Jefferson, *Notes on the State of Virginia,* Query VIII, reprinted in *The Writings of Thomas Jefferson,* Monticello Edition, vol. 1, ed. Andrew A. Lipscomb (The Thomas Jefferson Memorial Association, 1904) (1787), p. 124.

84 *where slavery was illegal*—Thomas Jefferson, in *The Papers of Thomas Jefferson,* vol. 10, ed. Julian Boyd (Princeton University Press, 1954), p. 296, editor's note. For a poignant, fictionalized account of this same paradox, see Max Byrd, *Jefferson* (Bantam, 1993), pp. 88–91.

85 *"disturbed in his possession"*—Thomas Jefferson to Paul Bentalou, August 25, 1786, in *The Papers of Thomas Jefferson,* vol. 10, p. 296.

85–86 *"these people are to be free"*—Thomas Jefferson, *Autobiography,* available at The Avalon Project, Yale Law School, http://www.yale.edu/lawweb/avalon/jeffauto.htm.

86 *together on equal terms*—Ibid. While Jefferson may have known he was doing wrong to his slaves by keeping them, he did not think he could do them much good by freeing them. In his view, the only solution to the problem of slavery was gradual emancipation coupled with deportation back to Africa. Any other plan would result in blacks' visiting a violent retribution on their former masters. "We have the wolf by the ear," he once told a friend, "and we can neither hold him, nor safely let him go." Letter to John Holmes, April 22, 1820, available at Thomas Jefferson Exhibition, Library of Congress, http://www.loc.gov/exhibits/jefferson/159.html. Racial differences, in other words, could never be sufficiently overcome so as to allow blacks and whites to enjoy equal rights.

86 *lines of distinction between them*—Thomas Jefferson,

Autobiography, available at The Avalon Project.

86 *"sensation than reflection"*—Jefferson, *Notes on the State of Virginia,* reprinted in *The Writings of Thomas Jefferson,* Monticello Edition, vol. 2, p. 194.

86 *art nor imagination*—Ibid., pp. 195–99.

85 *could not anticipate danger*—Ibid., p. 193–94.

86 *"over those of his species"*—Ibid., p. 193.

87 *"hypocrisy and meanness"*—The Virginia Act for Establishing Religious Freedom, 1779 draft, available at Religious Freedom Page, University of Virginia http://religiousfreedom.lib.virginia.edu/sacred/vaact_draft_1779.html.

88 *"coercions on either"*—Ibid.

88 *"Infidel of every denomination"*—Thomas Jefferson, *Autobiography,* available at The Avalon Project.

89 *"freely to contradict them"*—The Virginia Act for Establishing Religious Freedom, 1779 draft, available at Religious Freedom Page, University of Virginia http://religiousfreedom.lib.virginia.edu/sacred/vaact_draft_1779.html.

89 *"brain of Jupiter"*—Letter to John Adams, April 11, 1823, in Thomas Jefferson and John Adams, *The Adams-Jefferson Letters,* vol. 2, ed. Lester Cappon (University of North Carolina Press, 1959), p. 594. Kramnick and Moore collect many of Jefferson's antireligious statements in their work. Isaac Kramnick and R. Laurence Moore, *The Godless Constitution: The Case Against Religious Correctness* (W. W. Norton, 1996). For a lengthier listing of Jefferson's criticisms of religion, see John E. Remsberg, *Six Historic Americans: Paine, Jefferson, Washington, Franklin, Lincoln, Grant, the Fathers and Saviors of Our Republic, Freethinkers* (The Truth Seeker Company, 1906). The Remsberg book is instructive, but not entirely reliable.

89 *"and three heads"*—Letter to James Smith, December 8, 1822, in *The Writings of Thomas Jefferson,* Monticello Edition, vol. 14, pp. 408–9.

89 *"catch no more flies"*—Letter to John Adams, August 22, 1813, in *The Adams-Jefferson Letters,* vol. 2, p. 368.

89 "God of Israel"—*The Writings of Thomas Jefferson,* Monticello Edition, vol. 15, p. 260.

90 *"capricious, and unjust"*—Letter to William Short, August 4, 1820, in *The Writings of Thomas Jefferson,* Monticello

Edition, vol. 15, p. 260.

90 *"indifferent man with us"*—Letter to John Adams, April 8, 1816, in *The Adams-Jefferson Letters,* vol. 2, p. 468.

90 *"power to themselves"*—Letter to Samuel Kercheval, January 19, 1810, in *Thomas Jefferson: Writings,* ed. Merrill D. Peterson (Library of America, 1984), pp. 1214–15.

90 *"hollow of their hands"*—Letter to William Short, April 13, 1820, in *The Writings of Thomas Jefferson,* Monticello Edition, vol. 15, pp. 246–47.

90 *"approach of daylight"*—Letter to Jose Francesco Corre a Da Serra, April 11, 1820, in Thomas Jefferson, *Letters to and from Jefferson, 1820* (University of Virginia Library, 1996) (etext).

90 *"protection to his own"*—Letter to Horatio Spafford, March 17, 1814, in *The Writings of Thomas Jefferson,* Monticello Edition, vol. 15, p. 119.

90 *"claimed any other"*—Letter to Benjamin Rush, April 21, 1803, in *Thomas Jefferson: Writings,* ed. Peterson, p. 1122.

91 *"I am a Materialist"*—Letter to William Short, April 13, 1820, in *The Writings of Thomas Jefferson,* Monticello Edition, vol. 15, p. 90.

91 *"dragoons of Marat"*—Kramnick and Moore, *The Godless Constitution,* p. 89. Part of the original version was set in all-caps typeface; the emphasis has been removed for ease of reading.

91 *"and no God!!!"*—Ibid., p. 91. All-caps typeface has been normalized.

92 *"history and character"*—Letter to John Adams, May 5, 1817, in *The Adams-Jefferson Letters,* vol. 2, p. 91.

92 *"into public opinion"*—Letter to William Short, April 13, 1820, in *The Writings of Thomas Jefferson,* Monticello Edition, vol. 15, p. 246.

93 *kept from public ears*—See, for instance, Jefferson's letter to William Short, ibid. In it he enclosed a syllabus on his beliefs about Jesus' teachings, about which he remarked: "At the request of another friend, I had given [Benjamin Rush] a copy. He lent it to *his* friend to read, who copied it, and in a few months it appeared in the *Theological Magazine of London.* Happily that repository is scarcely known in this country, and the syllabus, therefore, is still a secret,

and in your hands I am sure it will continue so." Ibid., p. 92.

93 *"and a good thing, too"*—Kramnick and Moore, *The Godless Constitution*, p. 44.

Chapter 9: The Early First Amendment: A Disappointing Compromise

95 *America was arguing*—For an excellent discussion on the place of faith in the founding period, see Michael Novak, *On Two Wings: Humble Faith and Common Sense at the American Founding* (Encounter Books, 2001).

95 *"freedom of the press"*—Jefferson to Madison, December 20, 1787, in *Thomas Jefferson: Writings,* ed. Merrill D. Peterson (Library of America, 1984), pp. 915–16.

95 *"every government on earth"*—Jefferson to Madison, December 20, 1787, in *Jefferson: Writings,* ed. Peterson, p. 916.

96 *"in the requisite latitude"*—Madison to Jefferson, October 17, 1788, in James Madison and Thomas Jefferson, *The Republic of Letters,* ed. James Morton Smith (W. W. Norton, 1995), vol. 1, p. 564.

96 *"secure what we can"*—Jefferson to Madison, March 15, 1789, in *Jefferson: Writings,* ed. Peterson, p. 944.

97 *"any other pretense whatever"*—Articles of Confederation, Art. III, available at The Avalon Project, Yale Law School, http://www.yale.edu/lawweb/avalon/artconf.htm.

97 *Massachusetts merely required belief*—The Massachusetts Constitution, oddly enough, requires only that its governor be a Christian, and sets out the same oath requirement for other officials.

98 *"God blessed forevermore"*—Isaac Kramnick and R. Laurence Moore, *The Godless Constitution: The Case Against Religious Correctness* (W. W. Norton, 1996), p. 30.

98 *states forgo theirs*—Cf. Madison's statement that the constitution was opposed in New England because its ban on religious tests would open the doors to "Jews, Turks, & infidels."

99 *"in the fullest latitude"*—Madison to George Eve, January, 2, 1789, available at Philip B. Kurland and Ralph Lerner, *The Founders' Constitution* (University of Chicago Press,

1986), http://press-pubs.uchicago.edu/founders/documents/v1ch14s48.html.

99 *by 336 votes*—John T. Noonan Jr., *The Lustre of Our Country: The American Experience of Religious Freedom* (University of California Press, 1998), pp. 77–78.

99 *"on this one point"*—Bernard Schwartz, ed., *The Roots of the Bill of Rights* (Chelsea House Publishers, 1981), vol. 5, p. 1106.

100 *"maxims of free government"*—Noonan, *The Lustre of Our Country,* p. 77.

100 *"jury in criminal cases"*—Ibid., p. 79.

100 *rejected that proposal*—Ibid., p. 80.

100 *"established by law"*—Ibid.

100 *"free exercise thereof"*—U.S. Const. Amend. I..

100 *not to the states*—In his second inaugural address, Jefferson told the nation why he had refused to call a national day of prayer and thanksgiving. He explained that "In matters of religion, I have considered that its free exercise is placed by the Constitution independent of the powers of the General Government. I have therefore undertaken on no occasion to prescribe the religious exercises suited to it, but have left them, as the Constitution found them, under the direction and discipline of the church *or state authorities* acknowledged by the several religious societies." In other words, Jefferson's stated objection to a national day of prayer and thanksgiving was not so much that it threatened religious liberty, as that it threatened the right of the *states* to regulate religion as they saw fit. (Interestingly, it was Secretary of State James Madison who suggested to Jefferson that he admit that religion remained subject to state regulation. Jefferson's original draft contained no reference to the state governments, but Madison's proposed revision stated that the Constitution left religion "under the direction and discipline acknowledged within the several *States* [emphasis added]." *Republic of Letters,* vol. 3, p. 1364.

101 *"Constitution of the United States"*—*Permoli v. City of New Orleans,* 44 U.S. 589, 609 (1845). In 1833, the Supreme Court had decided *Barron v. Baltimore* in which the plaintiff, Barron, was suing the city of Baltimore, alleging that the city owed him "just compensation" under the Fifth Amendment's takings clause for having harmed his

property. Chief Justice John Marshall rejected this view, arguing that the restrictions on government power contained in the Bill of Rights applied only to the federal government. "The Constitution," he argued, "was ordained and established by the people of the United States for themselves, for their own government and not for the government of the individual States," and, therefore, "the Fifth Amendment must be understood as restraining the power of the general government, not as applicable to the States." 32 U.S. 243 (1833).

102 *"they may with practices"*—*Reynolds v. United States*, 98 U.S. 145, 166-7 (1879).

102 *"in the negative"*—James Madison, "Detached Memoranda" (1817), available at Philip B. Kurland and Ralph Lerner, *The Founders' Constitution* (University of Chicago Press, 1986), http://press-pubs.uchicago.edu/founders/documents/amendI_religions64.html.

103 *"inherent natural rights"*—George Washington's letter to the Touro Synagogue (1790). Photographs of the original and transcript available at George Washington Letter, Touro Synagogue, http://www.tourosynagogue.org/GWLetter1.php.

Chapter 10: In the States, the Aftermath of a Compromise

107 *"all...Roman-Catholics"*—Philip Hamburger, *Separation of Church and State* (Harvard University Press, 2002), p. 218. Another such group was known as the American Protective Association. An accurate picture of what it stood for can be taken from one of the oaths that all A.P.A. members would swear: "I do most solemnly promise and swear that I will always, to the utmost of my ability, labor, plead and wage a continuous warfare against ignorance and fanaticism; that I will use my utmost power to strike the shackles and chains of blind obedience to the Roman Catholic Church from the hampered and bound consciences of a priest-ridden and church-oppressed people; that I will never allow any one, a member of the Roman Catholic Church, to become a member of this order, I knowing him to be such; that I will use my influence to promote the interest of all Protestants everywhere in the world that I may be; that I will not employ a Roman Catholic in any capacity if I can procure

the services of a Protestant."

107 *"less than twenty-one years"*—John R. Mulkern, *The Know-Nothing Party in Massachusetts: The Rise and Fall of a People's Party* (Northeastern University Press 1990), p. 102.

107 *"Nunneries and Convents"*—Ibid., pp. 76–103.

107 *"pretence of loving liberty"*—Letter to Joshua Speed, in Abraham Lincoln, *Collected Works of Abraham Lincoln*, vol. 2, ed. Roy P. Basler (Rutgers University Press, 1953), pp. 320, 323.

108 *"exclusively of its own schools"*—Mass. Const. Amend Art. XVIII (superseded by Mass. Const. Amend. Art. XLVI).

108 *admitted to the Union*—See, *e.g.*, Act of Feb. 22, 1889, 25 Stat. 676, ch. 180 (1889) (enabling legislation for South Dakota, North Dakota, Montana and Washington). See also Eric Treene, *The Grand Finale Is Just the Beginning*, note 43, The Federalist Society White Papers, at http://fedsoc.org/pdf/FedSocBlaineWP.html.pdf.

109 *"out as prisoners"*—Reprinted in Jonathan D. Sarna, *Religion and State in the American Jewish Experience* (University of Notre Dame Press, 2000), p. 132.

109 *revoke the order*—Ibid., p. 131.

109 *"their precious rights"*—Ibid., p. 133.

110 *or practice law*—Morton Borden, *Jews, Turks and Infidels* (University of North Carolina Press, 1984), p. 37.

110 *"other religious sects"*—Sarna, *Religion and State*, p. 94.

110 *and "Judas Iscariot"*—Borden, *Jews, Turks and Infidels*, pp. 40–41.

110 *promptly voted it down*—Ibid., p. 37.

110 *political rights in the state*—Ibid., p. 40.

110 *Jews need not apply*—Ibid., p. 28.

110 *hold office until 1876*—Ibid., p. 34.

110 *in all states until 1877*—Sarna, *Religion and State*, p. 63.

Chapter 11: Where Does Religious Liberty Come From?

117 *"infringement of natural right"*—A Bill for Establishing Religious Freedom, in *Thomas Jefferson: Writings*, ed. Merrill D. Peterson (Library of America, 1984), pp. 347–48.

117 *human always and everywhere*—For an excellent discus-

sion of the shape of human nature and its impact upon religious liberty, see Stephen G. Post, *Human Nature and the Freedom of Public Religious Expression* (University of Notre Dame Press, 2003).

117 *"should be free"*—*Jefferson: Writings,* ed. Peterson, pp. 283–84.

119 *"to ourselves, we knowers"*—Friedrich Nietzsche, *On the Genealogy of Morality,* ed. Keith Ansell-Pearson (Cambridge University Press, 1994), p. 3.

Chapter 12: Personal, Not Private

126 *belongs only in private*—For excellent discussions of this problem, see Richard John Neuhaus, *The Naked Public Square: Religion and Democracy in America* (William B. Eerdmans Publishing Co., 1984); and Stephen L. Carter, *The Culture of Disbelief* (Anchor, 1994).

Chapter 13: The First Amendment at Midlife

131 *Rabbi Teitelbaum was among them*—According to Eichmann, Kastner "agreed to keep the Jews from resisting deportation—and even keep order in the camps—if I would close my eyes and let a few hundred or a few thousand young Jews emigrate illegally to Palestine. It was a good bargain." David Luban, "A Man Lost in the Gray Zone," *Law and History Review,* vol. 19 (2001), p. 161.

132 *remedial math and English classes*—*Aguilar v. Felton,* 473 U.S. 402 (1985).

134 *"without due process of law"*—U.S. Const. Amend. XIV.

135 *"liberty" in the due process clause*—See Akhil Reed Amar, "The Bill of Rights and the Fourteenth Amendment," *Yale Law Journal,* vol. 101 (1992), pp. 1194, 1233.

138 *teachers in religious schools*—*School Dist. v. Ball,* 473 U.S. 373 (1985).

138 *even for daily Mass*—*Zobrest v. Catalina Foothills School District,* 509 U.S. 1 (1993).

138 *for field trips*—*Wolman v. Walter,* 433 U.S. 229 (1977).

138 *religious school itself*—*Everson v. Board of Education,* 330 U.S. 1 (1947).

138 *but not maps*—*Meek v. Pittenger,* 421 U.S. 349 (1975); *Board of Education v. Allen,* 392 U.S. 236 (1968).

138 *"and twisted than I expected"*—*Zorach v. Clauson,* 343

U.S. 306, 325 (1952) (Jackson, dissenting).

138–39 *"and variable barrier"—Comm. for Pub. Educ. & Religious Liberty v. Regan,* 444 U.S. 646, 671 (1980) (Stevens, dissenting).

139 *"amorphous and distorted"—Bd. of Educ. of Kiryas Joel v. Grumet,* 512 U.S. 687, 720 (1994) (O'Connor, concurring).

139 *"unworkable in practice"—County of Allegheny v. ACLU,* 492 U.S. 573, 669 (1989) (Kennedy, concurring).

139 *"by any principle"—Kiryas Joel,* 512 U.S. at 751 (Scalia, dissenting).

140 *exercising her religion—Sherbert v. Verner,* 374 U.S. 398 (1963).

140 *"when a general law burdened":* I emphasize the words "general law" because those are treated differently from laws specifically targeted toward religion. See, for instance, *Church of Lukumi Babalu Aye v. City of Hialeah,* 508 U.S. 520 (1993), where the Supreme Court struck down a ban on ritual animal slaughter because it found that the ban was actually targeted to restricting a specific religious exercise.

140 *Employment Division v. Smith*—494 U.S. 872 (1990).

141 *Religious Freedom Restoration Act*—42 U.S. 2000bb (1993).

141 *Religious Land Use and Institutionalized Persons Act*—42 U.S. 2000cc (2000).

Chapter 14: The Right to Be Wrong

146 *the right to be wrong*—In more traditional terms, we could say that while there is no ultimate right we can assert against God Himself to hold erroneous beliefs, we are nonetheless entitled to be free from coercion by our fellow human beings.

Index

ACLU v. Sycamore Community School District, 26
Act for Suppressing Quakers (Virginia), 46
Act of Toleration (England), 59, 66, 71
Act of Toleration (Maryland), 59
Adams, John, 83, 89
Agostini v. Felton, 139
Aguilar v. Felton, 132, 139
Al-Jazeera, x, 145–46
American Party (Know-Nothings), 106–8
Amish, 1, 16, 54
Anglicans, 12, 13, 61, 74, 77
    see also Church of England
Articles of Confederation, 95
    religion and, 96–97
atheists, 66, 74, 110

Baptists, 63, 65, 71, 99
Becket Fund for Religious Liberty, ix, 17, 18, 26, 38, 125, 145
"Beginner's Bible case," 125–26
Bentalou, Paul, 85
Bill for Establishing Religious Freedom, 76–77, 80, 87–89, 92, 116
Bill of Rights, 51, 95, 99, 102, 134–37
Bingham, John, 135

Black, Hugo, 137–38
Blaine, James G., 108
Blaine Amendments, 107–8
Bonham v. District of Columbia Library Admin., 26
Bradford, William, 10, 13, 19, 22–24
Brindenbaugh v. O'Bannon, 26
Buddhism, 17, 112, 115

Calvert, Cecil, 58–59
Calvert, George, 58–59, 60
Carolina, 57, 64–66
    see also North Carolina; South Carolina
Catholics, 17, 57, 58–62, 66, 77, 91–92, 100, 110–11, 116, 137
    Nativists and, 105–8
China, 115, 116
Christmas, 22–24, 26, 128
Church of England, 10, 12, 13, 31, 33, 59, 65, 66
    separatists from, 10–11
Civil War, 51, 109
Clinton, Bill, 90
Connecticut, 110
conscience, 14, 15, 123–24
    defined, 121–22
    free will and, 120–22
    freedom of, 7, 32, 39, 42, 64, 74, 77, 87
    respect for, 15–18, 21

conscientious objection, 24,
    52–53
    Quakers and, 45–51
    in twentieth century, 52
Constitutional Convention, 97
Continental Congress, 47, 50, 53
Copeland, John, 40, 42
culture, 25, 126–28
    human nature and, 23–24,
    27–28
    religious expression and,
    12–13
culture war, 2, 5–6, 24–26, 146

Declaration of Independence,
    83–84, 93
Declaration of Rights (Virginia),
    72–76, 78, 100–1
Delaware, 51, 97
Douglas, William O., 137–38
Dwight, Timothy, 91
Dyer, Mary, 41-42, 88, 116

Easter, 4, 126
Eichmann, Adolf, 131
England, 10, 30, 39, 61, 101
    Act of Toleration, 66, 71
    Quakers in, 60
Employment Division v. *Smith,*
    140–41
establishment clause, 100–2,
    133–34
    incorporation, 137–39

Federalist Party, 90–91
First Amendment, 54, 96, 98–99
    free exercise clause, 100–2,
    106
    incorporation, 134–44
    and state law, 106, 111

Fourteenth Amendment, 134-36
    privileges and immunities
    clause, 135
Franklin, Benjamin, 83
free exercise, 59, 101
    origin of term, 78–80
free exercise clause, 100–2, 106
    incorporation, 140–41
freedom to preach, 30, 33, 39

Gandhi, Mohandas, 53–54
Ganulin v. *United States,* 26
Gedhun Choekyi Nyima, 115
Georgia, 17, 97
Ginsburg, Ruth Bader, 137–38
Glorious Revolution, 66
Godless Constitution, The,
    92–93
Good Friday, 25–26
Grant, Ulysses S., 109, 111
Granzier v. *Middleton,* 26
Gruber, Jacob, 135

Halloween, 4, 26
Hanukkah, 26, 128
Hawthorne, Nathanael, 30
Heller, Joseph, 52
Hemings, James, 84
Hemings, Sally, 84–85
Henrietta Maria, Princess, 58, 101
Henry, Patrick, 73, 77–78, 80, 99
Holder, Christopher, 40, 42
Hutchinson, Anne, 35–39

idiot/*idiotes* (defined), 126
incorporation doctrine, 134–36
    establishment clause and,
    137–39
    free exercise clause and,
    135–37, 140–44

Inner Light, 39, 41, 62
    conscience and, 40
Israël, 39

Jackson, Robert H., 138
Jamestown Settlement, 10
Jefferson, Thomas, 7, 76–77, 80,
    81, 106, 116, 137
    natural rights and, 95–96
    on religion, 88–92
    religious liberty and, 87–89
    slavery and, 83–87, 93,
    117
    on "wall of separation," 91
Jehovah's Witnesses, 54
Jews, 54, 62, 63–64, 66, 77,
    109, 131
    Jefferson on, 89–90
    "Jew bill" (Maryland), 110
    persecution of, 57, 59, 61,
    103, 108–11, 116, 137
    school accommodations,
    131–33
    state law on, 103, 109–11
Jordan, Thomas, 46

Kaskel, Cesar, 109
Kastner, Rudolf, 131
Kennedy, Anthony, 139
King, Martin Luther, Jr., 54
Kiryas Joel, 131–33, 134, 139,
    142, 143
"Know-Nothing" Party, 106–8

land use, 17–18, 141–42
    Cypress, CA, 18
    Grand Haven, MI, 18
Laughlin, Seth, 51
Leddra, William, 41
Leland, John, 99

Lincoln, Abraham, 51, 109
    on "Know-Nothings," 107
Locke, John, 57, 65, 74
    Constitution of Carolina, 65
    Letter Concerning Tolera-
    tion, 66
Lutherans, 61
Lyford, John, 12, 17

Madison, James, 7, 51, 71,
    102–3, 136, 137
    First Amendment and, 99,
    106
    free exercise and, 72,
    78–80, 101, 144
    natural rights and, 95–96,
    99, 103
    religious liberty and, 72,
    75, 93, 111
Maryland, 57, 58–60, 63, 74
    abolitionist preachers in, 135
    constitution of, 97, 111
    "Jew bill," 110
    Quakers in, 46, 49
Mason, George, 72
Massachusetts, 97
    Jews in, 110
    Know-Nothings in, 107–8
Massachusetts Bay Colony, 28,
    30–37, 63, 116
    proselytism in, 29–36
    Quakers in, 39–43, 49, 53
Mayflower, 1, 7, 11
Mayflower Compact, 11
    religious liberty and, 12
    self-government and, 12
McBride, Jesse, 135
"Memorial and Remonstrance
    Against Religious Assess-
    ments," 78–80

Mennonites, 61
Metzl v. *Leininger,* 25
More, Thomas, 46
Mormons, 101
Moynihan, Daniel Patrick, 138
Muslims, 66, 145–46

Nativists, 105–8
natural rights, 41–42, 75–76,
    78–80, 103
    legal rights and, 109,
    116–17
New Age, 3
New Hampshire, 51, 97, 110
New Jersey, 25, 97
New York (state), 51, 98,
    131–33
Nietzsche, Friedrich, 119
North Carolina, 97, 135
    Jews in, 111
    Quakers in, 47, 51
Notes on the State of Virginia
    (Jefferson), 84

oaths, 45–48
    accommodations for, 48,
    98
    atheists and, 66
    Quakers and, 45–48, 61
    religious objections to, 46
    religious persecution and,
    46–47, 110
O'Connor, Sandra Day, 138, 139

"Park Rangers," ix–x, 2–6,
    25–26, 37–38, 80, 92, 126,
    127–29, 137, 143
    absolute truth and, 5
    freedom and, 3
Penn, William, 60, 97
    Frame of Government,

60–61
    religious liberty and, 62
Pennsylvania, 57, 60–62, 63
    conscientious objection, 51
    constitution of, 97
    Quakers in, 47, 49–50
Permoli, Father, 100–1
Pilgrims, 1, 9–14, 21–24
    conscience and, 13–14
    proselytism and, 1
    religious liberty and, 12
    religious tolerance and, 1,
    13
    self-government and,
    11–12
    see also Plymouth Colony;
    Puritans
"Pilgrims" (metaphorical), ix–x,
    2, 6, 37–38, 80, 93, 129, 137,
    143
pluralism, 2, 15–18, 55, 130
    conscience and, 15–16, 18
    Mayflower and, 9, 11
    public expression and,
    126–27
Plymouth Brethren, 54
Plymouth Colony, 1, 9, 12–14,
    15, 17–18, 21–24, 34, 63
    Christmas in, 22–24
    pluralism in, 1
    Thanksgiving in, 22
Powell, Lewis, 138
proselytism, 7
    Bay Colony and, 29–36
    Plymouth and, 1
Providence (Rhode Island), 34, 63
public holidays, 4, 26, 128
    Plymouth's celebration of,
    22–23
    role of government and,
    129–30

public schools, 4–5, 26, 128,
132–33
    Bible reading in, 125–26
    Protestant teaching in,
    105–6, 107–8
Puritans, 10–14, 21–24, 29–37,
39, 96
    see also Pilgrims

Quakers, 1, 39–44, 57, 106, 122
    conscientious objection
    and, 45–51, 53
    Inner Light and, 39–41, 62
    oaths and, 45–48, 61
    persecution of, 46–47
    Revolutionary War and,
    47

"refuge colonies," 57–66
Rehnquist, William, 138
Reid, Richard, 54
relativism, 15, 129
religious expression, 42
    culture and, 12–13
    Plymouth and, 22–23
    private, 3–5, 79
    public, 4, 79, 125–26
Religious Freedom Restoration
Act (RFRA), 141–42
Religious Land Use and Institutionalized Persons Act
(RLUIPA), 141
religious liberty, 6, 16, 30, 42,
54, 66, 75
    human rights and, 116–17
    origin of, 117–24
religious persecution:
    Jews and, 57, 59, 61, 110
    Quakers and, 46–47, 110
    see also Catholics

religious pluralism. *See* pluralism
religious tests (for public office),
97–98, 110
religious tolerance, 7, 57–61, 63
    inherent rights and, 103
    Pilgrims, 10
    Roger Williams, 32–33,
    63–64
Reynolds, George, 101
Rhode Island, 36, 39, 57, 97,
62–64, 117
    conscientious objection, 51
    Quakers in, 47, 49
Robinson, William, 41
Rous, John, 40, 42

Saint Patrick's Day, 128
Saint Valentine's Day, 4–5, 26
Santeria, 17
Satmars, 131–33
Scalia, Antonin, 138, 139
secularism, 138
    and holidays, 4–5
Seventh-Day Adventists, 140
Shakespeare, William, 122
"Sherbert case," 140, 141
Shiva Linga, 3
slavery, 83–87
    abolitionist preachers, 135
    Jefferson and, 88–92
Smith, James, 89
South Carolina, 65–66, 97
state constitutions, 65–66, 97–98
    Blaine Amendments, 107–8
    established religions, 110,
    136–37
state law, 105–11
    and establishment clause,
    133–34
    and Fourteenth Amend-
    ment, 134–37

and Jews, 103, 109–11
    test oaths, 110
Stevens, John Paul, 138–39
Stevenson, Marmaduke, 41
Sullivan, Andrew, 5
Supreme Court, 54, 142
    conscientious objection
    and, 52
    establishment clause and,
    132–33
    free exercise clause and,
    101–2
    incorporation doctrine,
    134, 137–42
    on polygamy, 101–2
    on Santeria, 17

Teitelbaum, Yoel, 131
Tennessee, 111
Thomas, Clarence, 138
Touro Synagogue, 103
Twain, Mark, 119

U.S. Congress, 51, 99–102
    on Blaine Amendments,
    108
    and establishment clause,
    133, 136–37
    Fourteenth Amendment,
    134
    and free exercise clause,
    142

on polygamy, 101–2
    Religious Freedom Restora-
    tion Act, 141
U.S. Constitution, 48, 53, 92,
    96, 116
    Bill of Rights, 51, 99–102
    on religion, 98
    state power and, 109
    see also First Amendment;
    Fourth Amendment
U.S. Court of Appeals, 25–26,
    125
U.S. Department of Education,
    125
Utah Territory, 101

Vatican City State, 37
Vermont, 97, 110–11
Virginia, 71–80, 83, 98
    conscientious objection, 51
    Declaration of Rights,
    72–76
    Quakers in, 46–47

Washington, George, 47–48, 55,
    137
    on natural rights, 103
White, Byron, 138
Williams, Roger, 31–37, 39,
    63–64, 75, 88, 97, 111, 117,
    144
Winthrop, John, 28–30, 32–37,
    39